Dear Fear

Volume 3

10 Powerful Lessons On Living Your Best Life On The Other Side Of Fear

Tiana Patrice

This book is intended to push you from the place that fear is attempting to keep you bound. This book is intended to give you hope and position you for purpose. This book is not intended to provide financial, health or legal advice. Please seek the appropriate counsel for financial, health or legal matters.

ALL THINGS ARE
WORKING FOR
YOUR GOOD

Contents

For God hath not given us the spirit of fear; but of power, and of love, and of a sound mind.

2 Timothy 1:7 KJV

How To Use This Book

Welcome to the Global Book Series, Dear Fear. We are so excited to have you on this journey with us.

Dear Fear is more than just a book. It's a tool for your transformation and success on the other side of your fear. It is meant to transform your way of thinking, inspire you to dream bigger than you've ever dreamt, and give you the tools to take immediate action against your fear.

Aren't you ready to take action? Aren't you ready to stop allowing fear to keep you playing small and breathing in the air of mediocrity? You are bold. You are royal. You are deserving. You are excellent. And fear has no more power over your life.

Within the pages of this book you will find courageous letters & stories from women all over the world who stood up to the fear of their past to boldly step into their destiny. We encourage you to join us on this journey at www.dearfearbook. com/letter and write your own *Dear Fear* letter! There is so much power in the release!

Be sure to join the movement over at www.amillionfearlesstrong. org and invite 5 of your friends to join you. Together we are A Million Fearless Strong.

We are on a mission to liberate women from the fear that's holding them back in life, career and business. So join the movement!

FEARLESSLY
DECLARE
YOUR SUCCESS

A Message From The Visionary Author

Hello Fearless Leader,

I'm so grateful that you are deciding to embark on an exciting journey of activating your fearLESS and beginning to live your best life on the other side of fear. It's not always an easy one. But it's necessary. Your "New Thing" that God has for you is on the other side of your fear. Your Victory is on the other side of your fear. Your Winning Season is on the other side of your fear. You can't tell me that's not something to be excited about!! I'm amped up for you!

Why? Because I know what it feels like to be plagued by feelings of defeat, overwhelm and self-sabotaging thoughts. I know what it feels like to want to take the "leap" but you don't because you are unsure of what's on the other side. I know what it feels like to be your own worst critic. I get it. I know that fear is a consistent hustler and will hustle you out of your hopes and dreams, like the enemy coming in to kill, steal and destroy. But here is what I also know, I know that God has given you the provisions for the vision. I know that God didn't bring you this far to just leave you stranded without the tools, people, and resources to get you to your "New Thing". I know that on the other side of what fear is trying to keep you from is abundance, freedom, joy, and possibilities.; and it all belongs to you. Don't allow fear to keep you from your inheritance.

In this book, Dear Fear Volume 3, we have pulled together 10 brilliant women tell you their stories of how fear attempted to keep them shackled, but how God pulled them out. They are sharing their tools and strategies with you to reach back and pull you forward. If you ask them, they will tell you that this journey hasn't been easy. But it's been liberating, rewarding, and for many, provided healing and deliverance.

This book is a tool that's meant to be used. This is not just another book. Each story has a common thread that ties us all together, Fear. As you go through this book, I encourage you to get excited about what God is positioning you for on the other side of your fear.

Bigger and Better is HERE.

Your next level has so much power attached to it, and when you arrive there...nothing will look the same. Fear will try to convince you that your problems, issues, and past are much bigger than your WIN, but fear is a liar. Stretch through the pages of this book and grow into your next season. This book will teach you resilience, it will require you to grow, and that may be uncomfortable, but trust it. Trust the process and let the process position you. This is just the beginning. It is done.

With Love,
Tiana Patrice

Dear Fear, You Can't Have My Assignment

By Visionary Author, Tiana Patrice

Have you ever felt depleted from giving and giving but knew restoration was just around the corner?

Burnt out, but not counted out? Growing thin but not giving up?

I think that is an accurate description of most of my 2018. Can you relate?

For weeks I asked myself...what was my word to describe 2018.. to date I still don't know. I'm unsure I can wrap up that year in just one word. To be honest, 2018 was 365 days of an intense roller coaster ride of unleashed purpose with prayers for restoration.

Ok, let me paint a picture.

Imagine a balloon that is filled up to the max with air, and instead of bursting, it begins to allow the air to seep out. Why? Because the balloon knows the air is best used out...than in (even if that means deflation). The balloon knows that the air inside has purpose, and that purpose is for more than just the balloon. So the air inside...must. go.

The transition into 2018 began December of 2017. God planted me in a dark corner and I couldn't move. As much as I wanted to move, I couldn't. It was an uncomfortable place to be in, but

11

soon…I surrendered. He covered me up and told me to stay there, while He prepared other people, places and things for my sprouting.

He poured into me and watered me and I could feel the restoration. He began to resurrect areas of me that laid dormant and restored areas that had been used up from the previous year. He knew that greater was coming and I would need my strength. He knew that He had to decrease me, and give me more of Him and because of that He had to separate me from the world.

While I was planted, my roots began to grow deeper in Him. And eachroot that grew had a purpose. In this season, I learned to worship in spirit and in truth. My prayer life strengthened. I even managed to get my hands on some boxing gloves and I practiced my right hook, jab and learned how to fight with the word of God…Oh yeah…your girl was ready for whatever was on the other side.

Even in the darkness and covered from the world, His light beamed through and I felt the warmth of God's love. I glowed, I was Son kissed, and I felt His loving hand reaching and pulling me out. It was time. The sprouting had begun and I could move again. I gallantly paraded around as my purpose burst from the soil. The seed was planted, the vision was clear. It was time to produce. And I…was ready.

Balloon Filled.

And then BOOM! Suddenly permission was granted, and the purpose, like air in a balloon, that filled me up was ready to be released. It was time for me to build my new co-working company Women's CEO Alliance. At first I walked into doors that weren't big enough to hold the vision. The no's felt like daggers to my destiny (how many of you can relate to this) but they were only preparing me for the ultimate Yes.

And I was right. The doors that I was meant to enter, God's glory and anointing permeated throughout, and the people were waiting with unlimited Yes's to my requests. It was like nothing I had ever experienced, but God explained it was because of my obedience. (I need someone to catch that) And when I walked into those doors, my faith was strong, however I'd be lying if I didn't say that fear wasn't far behind and on some days, fear walked in first. (Can I just be honest?)

Fear began to whisper piercing thoughts of failure. "What if you fail? What if Dothan isn't ready for a co-working space designed for women"

And then fear brought doubt. "Who are you to bring this to Dothan? Remember where you come from, you'll never be successful at this"

But on the days that fear wouldn't stop knocking at the door, my faith would shove my insecurities to the side and remind me WHO gave this assignment to me.

Let me tell you about my God! Being the great God He is, He not only walked with me every day, but He also stood in the gap of my tomorrow, and left a light on for me to follow Him in. Every day I put on my shoes of faith, and I trusted God even when I didn't understand. I trusted God even when I couldn't always see. I trusted God even when I grew weary. I trusted God, even when fear tried to tie my shoe strings. I trusted God.

As I continued throughout the year, purpose continued to ooze from my pores, it glowed and it glistened, it attracted and it served...but the more it released, it bagged my eyes, jaded my days and drained my existence until many days all I could do was crawl up into a ball and rest in His arms. But the very next day, I would rise again. There was work to be done.

Balloon Seeping.

You see, many want the popularity of purpose but don't want thesacrifices that come with the light. And, while purpose is designed to lead you to destiny, many want to take the freeway. News flash, that's not how any of this works. The road is full of twists and turns and your plans won't always go as planned. The roads may be dark and you won't always know the next turn, but you must drive anyways.

Many want the crowd but don't realize that few will understand the purpose, pain, and the piercing of the releasing. Few will know of the internal shakings, awakenings and deliverance that will have to take place for the work to be done. But the work must get done.

And I worked, and I sowed, and I plowed, because the harvest thatwas coming was bigger than me. And while my hands became calloused and my eyes became tired, God continued to guide me and strengthened me when I became weary. Never taken my hand off the plow or looking back, as that would make me unfit for the Kingdom.

And in four short months, a watering hole in a dry place was produced. And many have come and gone, and many continue to come. Lives are changing, homes are elevating, minds are shifting, businesses are growing. And the Lord said, this is just the beginning, put back on your hard hat…the work has just begun.

Even now, whenI question the validity of the vision, (Because let's be honest, it's easy to do) God reminds me that people believed Noah to be crazy…but then the flood came. And so I continue to work, I continue to sow, and I continue to plow, because the harvest is just now feeling the warmth of the light.

There was no way I could wrap up 2018 with just one word. That year was the hardest most rewarding year of my life and business. And still…I was wife, mom, daughter, friend, coach and the leader of a movement against fear that is breaking generational curses, changing conversations, lifting families and more, while continuing to grow a profitable business. Occasionally I remembered to leave a little something for myself, many times I just got the leftovers.

And then once the balloon was deflated, God allowed it to float withered and jaded into the hands of people, that he made strong enough to carry it. And there they were, waiting to fill it back up with foundational, sustainable resources and air. I realized God allowed the balloon to deflate because the next release would only be from the overflow and the balloon would never run out of air again. I need somebody to catch that.

THE TRUTH ABOUT YOUR ASSIGNMENT IS…

While it is the most rewarding thing, it doesn't work unless you obey the instructions. Even afraid, you must obey the instructions and not deviate from God's plan. Understand that your purpose doesn't come easy, and it's not something you can "find". It's the thing that is already within you, that you need to get still enough to activate. It's the thing that is already within you that God graced you with. The reality is...

- Many want the life...but aren't ready for the sacrifices.

- Many want the crown...but don't want the ring of fire that comes with the crowning. (Come on now, that's a whole word!)

- Many want the harvest....but don't want to plant or even invest in the seeds.

- Many see the harvest but don't understand the tears that will have to water the soil.

I don't have one word.

That wouldn't help you at all.

Instead of one word...I'll share what I've learned on this journey in hopes that it can help you.

Why? Because on this journey my purpose is to help you identify your purpose possibilities, and empower you to take action on the other side of your fear. Understand that on this journey, life happens, crap happens, things happen! Roll with it. Don't allow it, to roll over you. Embrace your process and allow it to position you into your next.

1. *As you prepare for purpose, prepare for the attacks:*

On the outside the lights shine bright, and on the inside the bulb questionsitself and feels so alone. The reality is, as bright as your bulb burns, and as much of a light as you are, and will be…this is the very reason you will be attacked. You will be attacked mentally, spiritually,and financially…your brilliance will be attacked, your health, your family, and anything else you are connected too. Why?

Because what you are carrying is destined to change the world.

You feel alone because you are the one that's trusted to carry this mantle. No one else. The enemy wants you to feel invaluable, insignificant and unimportant, but that is only a lie to deceive you into opening your door to be robbed of everything God has instilled into you.

In this season you must learn to fight. Fight like your life depends…no fight because your life depends on it. Fight with the word of God. That is where you have everlasting strength. This confuses the enemy and he is no match for the power of the Lord.

2. Self care is more than a massage, but also asking for help:

The biggest trick of the enemy is making you believe weakness is a weakness. I really need someone to catch that. God said *when you are weak I am strong*. Baby trust me to be your strength! Ok God, I hear you.

The enemy wants you to be embarrassed about being weak so much that you don't even go to God for help. Don't be afraid to ask for help in areas that you are not strong in, this isn't just spiritually but in life, career, and business too. There are people whose destiny is connected to yours. Their harvest is wrapped up in the seed they plant into you. Don't block someone's harvest because you won't allow them to help you.

3. *Expect the separation and get excited about it:*

We have all heard the saying, with elevation comes separation. This is very true, however many of us think this is a negative thing. It's not. It's one of the best things that come with elevation. Elevation doesn't just separate you from people, but from your limited mindset that cannot take you to your destined place. You should be getting excited about that. Don't allow the enemy to keep you connected to a season you should have let go of a long time ago.

4. *Give from your overflow:*

Don't allow yourself to deplete and deflate from giving and giving.Make sure that you are surrounding yourself with people that can help you in your purpose, because the reality is, you can't do it alone. That means you are gonna have to trust someone, but Listen Linda, it's worth it.

Fill up your balloon, and keep it full. The air that seeps out, because the balloon is full, is what is meant for others. If you have ever flown before, the flight attendant always says…in case of emergency, put your mask on first, and then assist others. Make sure that you are making your self care a priority, because what good is purpose if you aren't well enough to pursue it.

RESTORATION IS HERE!

And Fear Has No Power Over What God Has Called Forth Within You.

I pray this year brings you complete restoration for everything thatGod released from you this year. I pray that He restores everything 10 fold and leaps you into your next season with an abundance of clarity, resources and prosperity. I pray that God overflows your bank account, your business, your career, your homes, your children, your movement and more. I pray that the next seed He plants in you is revealed and birthed into enlarged territories. I pray a complete renewal of your mind and complete destruction of your comfort zone. I pray that God allows you to hear what Heaven is saying about you and why you have been tasked with such a powerful purpose and graced with such a heavy anointing. And in all of this, I pray that God continues to allow you to produce and give from your overflow. Today, God is activating places in you that the enemy tried to lay dormant. Pivot into the purposed place God has for you. It's not easy. But it's rewarding and necessary. In Jesus name…Amen.

 I invite you to continue to join me on my journey as I war against fear, and serve purpose up on golden platters, dipped in the oil of our Father and strength of our ancestors while living the life I am destined to live. That totally sounded like Wakanda Forever lol. And I pray my journey empowers you and strengthens you to live your destined life too.

With Love,
Tiana Patrice

STOP ALLOWING FEAR
TO PUNK YOU OUT OF
YOUR DREAMS

YOUR
COMFORT ZONE
IS A TRAP

Chef Alesha Salahuddin

Dear Fear,

You are a thief and a liar! I let you rob me of my confidence, my peace, my joy, my truth, and my authority. It became normal for me to rely on you because you have been around for so long. In fact, you've been creeping around me and members of my family for generations. You tried to scare me into believing I couldn't do what God was leading me to do. I would overthink and second-guess myself, missing opportunities because of you! There were times when God wanted me to speak or make a move, but I would crouch down in fear. When God was telling me **YES**, I told Him **no** with my inaction because I was more comfortable with you than with HIM.

The attack on my health was the last straw. I surrender to the God I know and believe to be a HEALER! I am a queen and chosen by God. You can't have my testimony! This generational spirit of fear ends with me. I break the curse of fear, sickness, worry, doubt, and low self-esteem. I refuse to sit and watch you destroy the legacy of my bloodline. I'm rising up and standing in the gap for my family. In spite of what you tried to do to me and the lies I believed, God has a good plan for my life. His plans are still working for my good. This is my testimony. The story of my life is still unfolding.

I know you wanted me to fail, Fear. I have been your target since I was born---but even YOU can't stop the plan God has for my life! God's plans for my life have kept me on the side of VICTORY because I am a WINNER! So, I take back the authority that God gave me from the very beginning. I take ownership of my life…my blessed life. A life that has no limits. Never again, Fear, will you stop me from living the life I was born to live. I live my life now, full of confidence and fulfilling the purpose for which I have been called. I am enjoying my new way of living; by FAITH, trusting in JESUS (*the life-giver*). This is my testimony, my declaration to you, Fear…that I no longer have to be afraid.

Signed (With Confidence),
Alesha Y. Salahuddin

GET YOUR HOPES UP

Dear Fear,
You Can't Have My Testimony

William God allow certain things to happen in our lives that test our character; allow certain situations to take place in order for us to move forward? Will He allow circumstances, trials, and adversity to help get us get to where He needs us to be in life? Maybe He wants to use our testimony to help someone else? What about to help us overcome fear? I believe He does. I believe He tests us to refine us. God exposes our hearts through testing. The tragic and unforeseen situation I found myself in this past year was the last straw. It was the "now or never," for me Alesha Salahuddin, to turn her back and walk away from fear for good; to be the FEARLESS leader God called me to be.

In the spring of 2017, I found a large lump under my right armpit. It seemed to appear out of nowhere. I could feel it when I put my arm down close to my side. I was afraid something was wrong, so I called to set an appointment with my primary care doctor. He performed an examination and referred me to the breast care clinic for further evaluation.

A mammogram was conducted at my first appointment, leading to further imaging being needed in the form of an ultrasound and a biopsy. The doctors were not only concerned about the tumor found under my arm, but also a lump found in my right breast. Once testing was done, I was told it would take about two weeks to get the lab results. Of course, their concern was beginning to be my concern, but I let those anxious thoughts   26 subside. My husband and I had a scheduled trip to Puerto Rico, and I was determined to go and enjoy myself.

After our trip, I was called back in to get the results from the pathology report. The results showed that the abnormality tested in my right breast was benign, but "*__unable to determine__*" was written for the lump in the armpit area. Therefore, I was asked to schedule another biopsy to re-test that area. Now keep in mind, this procedure is called a core biopsy, where a large needle or core cuts a small piece out of the tumor to be sent for testing. This incision leaves you very sore for a few days until it heals. The radiologist asked me to do this test again in order to accurately determine if the tumor was benign or malignant. I reluctantly agreed.

I was alone for both appointments, and while lying there the second time, a wave of fear came over me.

I thought to myself, *What if something is wrong this time?* This wasn't my first mammogram. I had always made sure to schedule my exams because of my paternal grandmother's diagnosis of breast cancer back when I was a teen. I had this fear of having the same diagnosis. My exams had always produced positive results. I suppressed the negative feeling, reminding myself of the discussion I had with the doctor, where he assured me this procedure was an effort to ensure the tumor was well sampled in order to determine that nothing was wrong. I told myself, *You can do this. Everything is going to be alright.*

Both procedures were done with ultrasound to help guide the doctor in getting good samples of tissue from the tumor. The sound of the biopsy device reminded me of the sound a staple gun makes when it is in use. It was loud and several passes were done to make sure the tumor was well sampled. The tumor was measuring about 5 cm in diameter. I was bandaged up for the second time and told once again the sample would be sent to pathology for testing, but this time the wait wasn't as long as the first.

On June 21, 2017, my day of testing, or shall I say "the strengthening of my faith" had begun. It started out as a normal day. I am a personal chef, and I had just finished buying groceries to prepare meals for one of my clients. I was in route to his house when the phone call came in. I was approximately 7 miles from my client's home. The doctor who performed my last biopsy was on the other end. He asked how I was doing and said he wanted to discuss the results of the testing, but he could tell I was driving and wanted me to call when I had a moment. Hearing the tone of his voice, I asked him to tell me what he had to say right then, but he refused saying he was concerned about safety issues (another indication that the news wasn't good). I agreed to call him back, and we hung up. Of course, the last ten minutes of that drive was the worst as fear tried to rear its ugly head again.

I pulled into the garage of my client's apartment complex and parked my car. I couldn't get the groceries out of the car, loaded into my cart, onto the elevator, and into his apartment fast enough. I decided to put the items that needed refrigeration away first, while essentially trying to calm myself down. Then, I proceeded to call the doctor back. Another doctor answered the phone and took a message because my doctor had just stepped out with a patient. He said he would have him call me back in 15 minutes. The return call didn't seem to take that long, but the conversation from that call is what changed the course of my life forever. His voice was calm and gentle when I heard those infamous words, "You have breast cancer." He explained that the cancer had spread to my lymph nodes. Everything began to move fast from there. *I would get a phone call from this person…here's her name and number. I would need to meet with a team of doctors… go to this appointment…schedule that appointment.* It was crazy! When we hung up, I stood in place unable to move, frozen. I thought to myself, *What just happened?* Suddenly, I became paralyzed with fear.

My thoughts were everywhere. The anxiety I felt when the doctor first called had come back in full force. ***Did he just say I have breast cancer?*** I immediately thought of my family; my husband, children, and grandchildren. *Am I going to die?* All of these thoughts flashed across my mind. Once again, I was alone while trying to deal with these agonizing thoughts. I could feel the tears streaming down my face. A feeling of uneasiness came over me. Why is this happening to me? I had just started my personal chef business. My oldest son had recently gotten married and our 5th grandchild was on the way. I tried to imagine telling my husband, who happens to be my high school sweetheart, love of my life, and biggest supporter. We had created so many memories together and were looking forward to celebrating many more. I hurriedly pulled myself together because the phone calls from the hospital were starting to come in.

The first call was from the nurse navigator, introducing herself and explaining her role on the team. Initially, I decided to wait to call my husband. I thought he needed to hear news like this in person. But in less than an hour, I had appointments for a breast MRI, lab work, a chest x-ray, a genetics consult, surgery for port placement, and an appointment to meet with the team of doctors who would be in charge of my care. Once I got off the phone, I realized these appointments were to start as early as the next day, so I would have to inform my husband immediately so he would have time to rearrange his schedule. I knew he would want to be there with me.

I remember a long silence on the other end after I told him the news. He began by asking me a few questions, got the dates and times for my upcoming appointments, told me he loved me and that everything was going to be alright. We hung up. I felt better after I talked to him and was glad I did not wait to call. I remember him calling midday to check on me and make sure I was good. I put on my music (my usual when I'm cooking), finished my client's meals, cleaned up, and left the apartment. On my way home, I called my husband and he asked when I wanted to tell our kids. I wanted to gather my thoughts and at least attend the first appointment (scheduled for the next day) in order to have more information to give them. We agreed that would be best. A conference call with my family was scheduled for the following day.

A breast cancer diagnosis will not only take its toll on the patient but can affect those closest to them as well. There were times when my children felt frightened, worried, and angry as they watched me endure this grueling disease. I went through six rounds of chemotherapy, a sentinel node biopsy (which is surgery to remove the infected lymph nodes), and targeted therapy infusions for a year. I lost my hair, my appetite, weight, and my sense of taste. My body was progressively bombarded with sluggishness and fatigue. I had constant diarrhea, joint pain, and occasional mouth sores. I worried about my appearance and what others would think of me. I went through bouts of fear, frustration, discouragement, and even depression. Chemotherapy and other treatments cancer patients receive affects our immune system in powerful ways that influence our ability to fight.

My vain attempts at giving up prompted my husband's encouragement early on not to let myself go into a depression over a temporary situation. I was frustrated because my life, as I knew it, had been altered. I had to let go of clients because I could no longer stand for long periods of time. My low energy days outnumbered the days I had energy. The side effects of chemotherapy were trying to strip me of everything I had. Being forced to lie down was not something I was used to, but I found out that sometimes the best way to be productive is through REST. God will put you in a place of stillness in order to restore you and move you forward. It was part of the journey of "strengthening my faith."

My coping mechanisms began through writing. As I listened to the music I had downloaded to my playlist (aptly named **Strength of a Woman**, created to have while sitting through hours of chemo), I would write. I heard God speak through many of the songs I listened to. I began to use praise as my weapon toward healing. Writing became therapeutic for me. I wrote words of affirmation on my bathroom mirror that I could see and read every day. I would wake up early to pray and read. I wrote in my journal about one scripture in particular that I read on the day of my 1st chemo infusion.

"I can do all things [which He has called me to do] through Him who strengthens and empowers me [to fulfill His purpose—I am self-sufficient in Christ's sufficiency; I am ready for anything and equal to anything through Him who infuses me with inner strength and confident peace]." **(Phil 4:13 AMP)**

This scripture gave me the confidence and peace to go to the rest of my infusion appointments without fear. As I look back at some of the entries recorded at the start of my journey, I can see where I was signing off with *#blessed, #survivor, #fearless*. I was declaring positive energy over my situation from the very beginning. But at some point, I had given up writing for a while out of frustration with my process.

During a period of rest, God took me back to those journal entries. From there, I became determined to get better in spite of the toll the process was taking on my body. I worked out and took long walks when my energy levels were up. I went back to my love of cooking and tried new recipes. Many people reached out with acts of love and encouragement. I got out of the house with family and friends and took short trips to various places. I began to laugh again and force myself to enjoy the moments. I even set a goal early on (during one of my low energy days) that once I made it through chemotherapy, I wanted to go to New Orleans for the first time to celebrate my birthday and Mardi Gras in February. My husband promised to make the trip happen.

I was scheduled for surgery at the beginning of the year. Once complete, I received word from my surgeon that the tumor had responded well to treatment. A copy of the pathology report I received read, *"no evidence of cancer found"* in the lymph nodes removed. Everything seemed to be going well. The uphill battle was finally over, or so I thought. We made it to New Orleans as planned. For two first-timers in NOLA, we had a ball attending parades, dining on the city's famous Creole cuisine, attending the premiere of the blockbuster movie Black Panther, and taking in a concert to see Mary J. Blige. We danced in the streets during Mardi Gras, met new friends, rode bikes in the park, and took a late night stroll to Café Du Monde for their famous beignets. The night before we were due to leave is when things changed.

Back at the hotel room, I began experiencing pain in my left arm, which eventually transitioned to my upper back, neck, and shoulder area. I was in such excruciating pain by the time we arrived home, that I decided to go to the emergency room. At this point, the pain was affecting my range of motion. I began experiencing severe headaches and chills. I had a fever that had spiked to over 102°F. I was admitted to the hospital, and thus began a three-week stay and the FIGHT for my life. Just as I was getting to the point of overcoming one battle, healing through that process, and focusing on the "what's next" for my life, another obstacle; another attack on my body was taking place. I thought I was going to die. I was in so much pain, I literally thought I was going to die! A comparison of the blood cultures drawn from my port and arm revealed a staph infection on the port. I had contracted MSSA bacteremia that had begun spreading to other parts of my body. Further testing revealed internal jugular vein thrombosis, which essentially is a blood clot that developed in the left side of my neck near my collarbone; the same side the port was on. In addition, my breathing had become labored and tests revealed some fluid had developed in one of my lungs. Emergency surgery was performed to remove the infected port and a PICC line was inserted in my right arm in order to administer a 6 week supply of antibiotics.

I had never experienced a lengthy stay in a hospital before. Honestly, I had come to dislike the thought of having to stay in one because my mother passed away in the hospital six years prior. As a matter of fact, the last time she was admitted happened to be in the month of February as well. As I was lying in the hospital bed a couple of days after being admitted, weak and still in excruciating pain, I began to think of her. She was diagnosed with uterine cancer in the fall of 2011 and a complete hysterectomy was performed. She had dealt with symptoms of the diagnosis silently for months before she told me. I remember having to coax her into getting checked. After the surgery, the doctors wanted to treat her further with chemotherapy and radiation. Her white blood cell counts continued to stay high, which caused her body to weaken and delay treatment. No one knew, at the time, that she too was suffering from a bacterial infection. I didn't find out until after her death when I read the "cause of death" on her certificate.

I tell the story of my mom, comparing the similarities of her fight to mine because the strangest thing began happening to me during my stay in the hospital. One day, while the doctors made their rounds, they began with their usual series of questions. The voice I heard coming out of my mouth literally sounded like my mom. It was the weirdest thing! I'm sure you're thinking, *What's wrong with that?* The reason I became alarmed at my "*mom sounding voice*" is that I was in her hospital room, standing at the foot of her bed when she said out loud (*barely able to talk*) that **she was ready to go**. My husband and one of my cousins can testify with me regarding this moment. I tried not to let anyone see the fear and sadness I immediately felt as I took her hand in mine and asked her to pray with me. The uneasy feeling stemmed from the fact that I knew exactly what she meant. After three weeks in the hospital, she gained her angel wings on March 7, 2012.

Later on, I was shocked to learn that my husband and oldest son had heard the "*mom sounding voice*" as well. It made my husband so emotional that he stepped out of the room and called his sister for support through prayer. His greatest fear was that I was giving up and ready to go like my mom. I had lost a tremendous amount of weight. He saw me lying there *lifeless*, and thought what he saw happen to her was now happening to me.

As I was lying in that hospital bed, I thought about the journey I had been on. The fear that arose from the breast cancer diagnosis was now magnified by the news of the port infection. The enemy of my soul kept baiting me to give up, let go and just die. I began thinking about how my mom had passed away with a similar diagnosis to mine. My grandmothers and my aunt all had grueling illnesses prior to their death. These were all women I was very close to and who had been so supportive of me. *Was it time for me to go as well?* Death is final. Once it is over, it's over. There is no turning back.

After I was released from the hospital, I set out on a new journey of total healing. During my healing process from the infection, I learned that total healing encompasses so much more than our physical bodies. There are spiritual and emotional aspects of healing that are just as important. For example, I realized I had trouble with vulnerability. I was afraid to allow myself to trust completely. I needed to accept the things that took place in my childhood (that were beyond my control), let them go and forgive.

And I was unfortunately still grieving the loss of my beloved mother. These are some of the many things I plan to discuss further in a planned memoir/testimony of my life. I learned to release those issues and truly forgive because it was not only hindering my healing process but hindering my FREEDOM! I had to hit the reset button in my life in order to heal, in order to receive total forgiveness, total restoration, total healing, and total freedom.

Did you catch that? I hope so because it was so important to me during my healing process. The cancer diagnosis not only helped me come to terms with my life and the changes that needed to take place but also my faith and trust in God. I now walk in complete and total surrender to HIM. Fear tried to take the life that God gave me; a life of purpose, ministry, and inspiration. The scars I carry now are a constant reminder of how fear tried to escalate and overtake me, causing me to think I was going to die. I am constantly reminding myself of my greater purpose.

Fear is a tool used to keep people from enjoying their lives and making progress. I fought so hard to live because I knew it was not time for me to die. I know that if I let fear win, I will never experience God's perfect plan for my life. My abundance of blessings can only be received from God through FAITH. I am at peace with the journey God has placed me on. In essence, I have decided to tell cancer, ***"thank you"*** because the diagnosis only made me stronger and more determined to WIN. I am a cancer survivor still "thriving" under God's amazing GRACE!

1. **What offenses have you suffered that are hindering your ability to forgive yourself and others? Forgiveness is our way to FREEDOM. We can't get freedom without *FORGIVENESS*.**

_____

_____

_____

_____

_____

2. What are some ways that you can set aside time for yourself (physically, spiritually, mentally, and emotionally) to ensure your God-given vessel (*mind, body, and soul*) is healthy? Think of areas in your life that need improvement and begin working on those areas today.

_____

_____

_____

_____

_____

STOP QUESTIONING
YOUR FAVOR

Bio

Alesha Salahuddin is a Personal Chef who lives in the DC-Metro area. She is the owner of Silver Platter Cuisine, LLC, where she is currently realizing her dream of becoming a business owner and providing various services as a personal chef. In addition, she works part-time as a Culinary Instructor at Columbia College in Vienna, VA. Both endeavors allow her to share love and passion for all things culinary. Alesha is a graduate of Le Cordon Bleu, where she received her Bachelor of Arts in Culinary Management. She is a member of the United States Personal Chef Association where she serves as Treasurer of the DC-Capital Chefs Chapter.

Alesha has been married for 28 years to her high school sweetheart. She has raised 4 children and carries the loss of her 2nd child in her heart. She enjoys spending time with her 5 grandchildren. Born in Hampton, VA and raised (primarily) in Fayetteville, NC, she has been a part of the military community most of her life. Her husband served 25 years in the US Army, which afforded her and her family the opportunity to live overseas in Japan and various stateside locations. Alesha has always understood the importance and value of family and friendship. During her tenure as a military spouse, she was widely known for her gift of ministry in hospitality.

Her recent battle with breast cancer helped her realize her new motto *"Every Day is a Gift."* She has accepted this journey as another chapter to her amazing story, which continues to evolve and testify of God's grace of perseverance and overcoming in her life. She's excited about her newfound opportunity of authorship allowing her to be the fearless leader God has created her to be and to express a sense of transparency never seen before. She believes as she continually takes bold steps toward God's plan for her life that she will encourage others to be overcome by the words of her testimony.

www.silverplattercuisine.com

Search YouTube:

Alesha's Journey; Cancer Survivor:
https://youtu.be/npBoLYtLlp0

BOLDLY SPEAK WHAT YOU WANT TO SEE

Deborah Porter

Dear Fear,

Well, I will say this about you. You are nothing if not consistent. Your ability to always get back up when I think I've knocked you out is quite remarkable. In your presence, I have felt small and irrelevant.

You've convinced me, at times, that my best option is to just forget about it. Forget about opening up, forget about showing up, forget about sharing the deep stuff. "Just stay on the surface," you've whispered. "They won't understand, and in fact, will probably think less of you if they knew." I can look back and remember giving space, room, and an ear to entertain what you thought. I remember days I even sought out your counsel on what to do, how to do, and what to say. But every time, I walked away knowing I had relinquished a little bit more of myself. And then, I had the idea that choosing unforgiveness somehow put me in the driver's seat, gave me power, made me bigger, better. Just foolishness.

For a while I went along with you, high-fiving all the way. And then I was confronted with the one situation that would reveal to me the truth of who you are and how following you would not just impact me, but potentially future generations. I will now say this, you were wrong. My power, my voice, and my forgiveness do not need your permission to operate. That's right, Fear. I don't need you to co-sign on anything. In fact, I've decided to agree with the word of God once and for all on this. 2 Timothy 1:7 says, "For I've not given you a spirit of fear, but of power of love and of self-discipline." And here's the scripture that brought it home. I John 4:18, "There is no fear in love. But perfect love drives out fear, because fear has to do with punishment. The one who fears is not made perfect in love." So, I'm done with you Fear. I'm just done! You've confused me long enough. It's not courage that defeats you. It's not strength that wins out over you. It's love. Love drives you out. So, I choose to love, in spite of, because of, in lieu of. I CHOOSE LOVE!

Freedom feels good,
Deborah Porter

STOP ALLOWING FEAR
TO BE YOUR GPS

GOD ALREADY GAVE
YOU PERMISSION

Dear Fear,
You Can't Have My Forgiveness

Growing up in a safe little town, 15 miles outside of New York City was the best of all worlds. Often times we'd go to bed and forget to lock the front door. It was a town where everyone knew everyone, and any parent was allowed (and actually expected) to correct you. Things were simple; high school basketball games, cheerleading, sitting out on the stoop while getting your hair braided, drinking an orange soda without anyone being concerned about the red 40 dye or high fructose corn syrup it contained. The kind of place where you left home to go play and came home when the street lights came on. There were no cell phones, tracking devices or anyone knowing where you were. Because of that, some of those lazy summer days (and nights) my friends and I found ourselves on the 30-minute train ride into the city that never sleeps. A city so nice they had to name it twice, New York, New York. A simple walk around Harlem in the late '70s and early '80s was exciting. There were vendors on every corner, incense, music tapes, dashikis, you name it. Anything was available as long as you named the right price. We never really noticed the blocks of abandoned buildings that provided a backdrop for our adventure. Nights spent at clubs in midtown were an entirely different event. After school or work on a Friday afternoon, a nap was necessary because the party at the clubs didn't really get going until midnight, so the 11:19 pm train into Grand Central Station was the one to never miss.

None of us worried about much. Most of us had hard-working moms making sure we had what we needed, and whenever and however possible, what we wanted. A few of us had a mom and a dad making it happen, but that wasn't my story. My father was gone by the time I was born. My mom worked hard providing for my sister and I. But my Nana was my north star. I was blessed to have her unconditional love and care. She was my before and after school caregiver and so much more. I remember faking sick on school days so I could spend the whole day with her. I've heard people say "you can't miss what you've never known." Although that may be true about some things, I'm not sure it's true about everything. Growing up without my dad being present, I had lingering questions. *Why? Why aren't you here? Was it something I did?* Wanting those answers left me wondering at times. *What if he shows up to the school recital or cheerleading competition?* All the while I knew there was no way he would be there. So although life was good, as a child of a single parent, I grew up knowing that I would be the one responsible for my future. I grew up believing that depending on people would be the quickest way to being let down.

There was one person I could always depend on; me. I had to decide where I would go, how I would get there, if I were to succeed. It was no one else's job to achieve that but my own, and if I didn't, there would be no one to blame. So much of my motivation was fueled by fear. The fear of failure, the fear of rejection, the fear of no one being there to celebrate the successes. As senior year in high school rolled around, I realized I hadn't been very serious about my studies. I was a good, solid student but with more effort, I could've been a great student. One other thing started to bubble up inside of me in these later high school years. *I wonder where my dad is and what he's doing.*

But then it would be time for cheerleading practice, college applications, work or something else sufficient enough to shift my focus.

After graduating, I headed south for college. I knew if I stayed closer to home, NYC would draw me in every weekend. Although I found my stride academically, I struggled relationally. I didn't realize it then, but looking back it couldn't be any clearer. The dynamics of a healthy male/female relationship, that may have been easy for some, was as difficult as grasping water for me. There were friendships that suffered because of my inability to be vulnerable and authentic. It was easier to not allow anyone too close. I managed the hurt better that way. My 54-year-old self is quite clear about that now, but my 21-year-old self just thought this is how it is, and even more devastating, how it will always be.

At the age of 21, I knew that I had to get to the root of this. I was home from college for Christmas break, and after a series of events, had a conversation with my mom about meeting my dad. The necessary calls were made and the date and time were secured. He'd be picking me up for dinner in a couple of weeks just before heading back to Virginia for school. I remember laying in bed that night thinking, *What in the world have you done? You don't know him, he doesn't know you. What will you talk about? In fact, what will you call him?* So then I thought about reverting to my childhood excuse when I didn't want to do something. "Mommy, my stomach hurts!" I know it's ridiculous, but that's all I had at the moment. I must have fallen asleep because I woke up the next day with a new plan. I *want* to see him. I *want* him to see what he's missed, the fact that I had sloppily navigated all these years and relationships without him and was fine. I'm fine! We'll do this one-time meetup thing, I'll get some questions answered and that will be the end of that. Case closed. The evening came and my stomach didn't hurt, but there were about 3.4 million butterflies that had taken up residence. The doorbell rang and the person that came through it was the other piece of who I am. I remember us embracing, I remember him touching my face and I remember being completely overwhelmed. I've always been guarded with my emotions and deep thoughts. There was no way I was going to open up and share what I was really feeling with... with my....with him.

We went to dinner and had pleasant conversation, a typical conversation you'd have with anyone you're just meeting. As we pulled up to my mom's house, he asked if we could get together once more before I went back to school. Well, I have things to do, other people to see. I have to get back to the city at least once more before leaving, but I heard what sounded like my voice saying, "Sure!"

It was at the end of that second visit that I heard the words I didn't know I needed to hear, "I'm sorry." There was more detail and emotion with it, but it was definite, clear and unmistakable. And it was in no way requiring an acceptance. It was a statement. I remember walking into the house and my mom asking how dinner and the visit went. I gave the typical answer, "Fine." But really, it was remarkable. I felt something lift off of me that night. Maybe it was the chip on my shoulder I had been carrying named unforgiveness or maybe it was the weight of wondering if he knew I needed to hear that. Either way, from that night forward I felt lighter.

As the years went on, we developed a pleasant relationship. I met extended family on my dad's side and we stay in touch. Nothing too deep, but it's good. Then, the next big thing happened. The man I didn't know to ask God for, the absolute gift that God's given me, my future husband Clif asked me to become his wife! I'm elated, in love, engaged. But because my brain doesn't know how to shut itself off, while laying in bed looking at my engagement ring, fear returns. *Will he stay with me forever? What if he doesn't **really** love me?* Because at this point in my life, I knew love to be simply a feeling as opposed to a decision, a commitment. Which, often times, is not based on feeling alone. *Are you gonna ask him to walk you down the aisle?* In my head, I'm still referring to my dad as "him." It is at this moment that I begin to consult with fear on how to handle my dad and our relationship. Mind you, I've not responded to his offer of an apology from years ago. Partly because so much time has gone by and partly because I didn't want to. I felt I had a right to hold on to unforgiveness. So, fear and I began an alliance.

Fear had always been there, and I had given into it often over the years, but I always thought it was normal, harmless in a way. Fear of scary movies, which I still have. Fear of new things, people, places. But as I got older there was an increase in the fear of being me. Would it work out? Would I be accepted? Would I be enough? What if it failed...I failed? Ugh! I just can't seem to shut my brain off. As a senior in college, I received one job rejection letter after another, and soon realized I couldn't pull off this thing called life on my own. Those rejection letters brought back that familiar feeling I had as a child. For me, rejection traveled with two companions; incompleteness and defensiveness. I later realized that defensiveness is a front that sensitive people use to act as though nothing bothers us. Although I was afraid of what the future had for me, my best friend's parents (and my Nana, who was long gone) made sure we knew who holds our future. In that moment of fear, I surrendered to His plan for me. "Lord,

I don't know what to do. I'm living a facade. I need you!" I've heard it said that we all have a hole in our hearts the size of our Heavenly Father. The realization hit that I had 2 of those holes. One for each of my fathers. And it was my Heavenly Father who taught me how to begin the process of forgiveness.

I knew I had some work to do, I still do. It's the kind of work that's inward that you're never really finished with. I had to tackle what I believed was my right to not forgive. It became clear that I had to forgive my father if I expected to be forgiven. I had to unlearn that forgiveness is a sign of weakness. Somewhere along the way, I picked that up. Well, it was now time to throw it down.

Some 29 years ago, my dad walked me down the aisle. It was 1989, when big shoulder pads and asymmetric haircuts were a real thing, and I wore both that day. In later years, one of my children went to college just a few miles from where my dad lived, and as a result, my children know their grandfather in a way I didn't at their age. I am overjoyed that unforgiveness didn't win. I didn't realize it then, but fear has the ability to impact more than one generation.

So here is some of what I've learned and continue to learn. Forgiveness is not a one-time thing. It's mine to choose daily or even by the moment depending on the day or the offense. I have to choose it, put it on and wear it like a red blazer. There's nothing magical about it. It doesn't come down from the heavens and rest on me and voila, you're walking in forgiveness. You have to move toward it, exchange it for what you are feeling, and you do it as often as you have to in order to maintain it. Peter asked Jesus in Matthew 18:21, "How many times do I forgive, 7?" I'm sure he wasn't expecting the answer, 70 times 7! Forgiveness requires talking to yourself. When the offense comes to mind, you have to remind yourself (out loud if necessary), "No, I've already offered forgiveness of that. That's old, it's done."

What happens if I don't choose forgiveness? By default, I'm automatically choosing punishment, blame, a grudge, retaliation, bitterness. Guess who gets hurt by all of that poison? Not the person I'm not forgiving, but me! There is inward unrest when we allow ourselves to walk in unforgiveness. And as much as we all deserve forgiveness, we also deserve peace. Whether or not I wanted to admit it, peace was eluding me. Being vulnerable was not something I enjoyed, so I tried to avoid it as much as possible. And if I'm being honest, it's still not one of my favorite things to do. Why? Because there's a surrendering of control when you're vulnerable, and in my world, that meant you were weak. But I had reached the point that my way wasn't working. Not even a little bit.

This chapter started with a Dear Fear letter, but it will end with a Dear Daughter declaration. I have a series of letters written to me by my Heavenly Father and you do too. The word of God became the fuel and the source of forgiveness and the extinguisher of fear. I'm on a life's journey to walk out forgiveness. Even as I type that, fear suggested that I hit the delete button. *You can't say that. What if you mess up, what if it doesn't work out?* One thing is for sure, fear is on the job, but so am I.

GIVE FROM YOUR
OVERFLOW

THERE'S A BLESSING IN THE STRETCHING

DEAR DAUGHTER,

I have loved you with an everlasting love. I give you strength when you are weary. Do not fear, daughter, I am with you. No weapon formed against you will prosper. I will go before you and never leave nor forsake you.

Dear Deborah, I know the plans I have for you, plans to prosper you and not harm you, plans to give you hope and a future.

I'll leave you with this, a broken heart can heal, love outlasts and overpowers fear, and offering forgiveness doesn't mean you're weak. In fact, it just might be your superpower. Sometimes, the first step toward forgiveness is forgiving yourself. Forgiving yourself for not letting others in, building the wall of protection so thick that it actually becomes a prison and not a place of protection. Or it may be the opposite, letting everyone in with no boundaries at all. Once you've forgiven yourself, who is the person you need to freely forgive? Are you able to offer it even as a trickle? Maybe you're ready to be extravagant with your forgiveness and let it flow without obstruction. Remember, your freedom is attached to the forgiveness, not the apology.

1. **What do you need to forgive yourself of? Don't hold back, you're worthy of forgiveness.**

_____

_____

_____

_____

_____

2. Who do I need to extend forgiveness to with no strings attached? What is the first action step I can take toward that decision?

_____

_____

_____

_____

_____

BROKEN CRAYONS
STILL COLOR

Bio

Deborah is a devoted wife and mother of 3 adult children. She is a native New Yorker at heart and was born and raised in Westchester County. Deborah left for Virginia in the early 1980s to attend college. She graduated from Virginia Commonwealth University (VCU) where she met her husband, Clifton, with a BS in the Administration of Justice and Public Safety. Deborah worked as a Criminal Investigator and Probation Officer in the state of Virginia from the mid '80s to the early '90s.

The decision to be a stay at home mother was made after much prayer and many conversations with her husband, Clifton. They didn't realize it then, but it would be one of the best decisions they would make. During those years, Deborah became a community volunteer in each city they lived in. A recurring pattern for Deborah was the role of a mentor. After having many women mentor her, starting with her grandmother, Mildred Murray, she quickly realized the importance of being poured into while simultaneously pouring into others.

Deborah believes in and is thankful for the ministry of the local church. Much of her leadership and mentoring skills were refined there. She has experience leading women's ministries, children's ministries, at-home mom groups, marriage small groups with her husband, Clifton, and high school mentoring programs to name a few. She believes there is no substitute for a relationship with Jesus Christ and allowing Him to lead.

One of her favorite quotes is, "Jesus has called us to be fishers of men, not cleaners of fish." She believes the word of God from cover to cover.

Currently, Deborah has started the Moms Mentoring Circle to continue supporting others. She mentors at-home moms with systems for themselves, their families and their home. She also volunteers at the National Museum of African American History and Culture in Visitor Services, while also mentoring new volunteers. She and her husband, Clifton, serve together with the VCU African American Alumni Mentoring Program. The program helps to pair undergraduate students with alumni in similar fields of study. For more info about either program, please email deborah@deborahporter.net.

Deborah and Clifton have been married for over 29 years. They currently reside in Alexandria, VA and enjoy spending time in Naples, FL. Two of their children, Chanel (27) and Christian (24) reside in Harlem, NY and their youngest son, Clif (JoJo) is a senior at Villanova University.

YOU ARE WORTH
IT & YOU
MATTER

Carla Ricks

Dear Fear,

You can no longer consume my thoughts and allow me to get frustrated with the inevitable occurrences associated with life. You try to convince me that I can't have it all and that I can't be the person I've always dreamed of becoming. You want me to believe that I can't be a good mother and have a happy marriage; progress successfully in a career; be a dependable, loyal, caring and fun daughter, sister, and friend, all while maintaining a healthy physical and financial lifestyle. You want me to believe that one of those things will have to give and that I'm trying to do too much. You want me to get consumed with frustration and anxiety every time a situation occurs that conflicts with my heart's desire of being those things. You want me to get upset with those around me and pit one desire against the other in an effort to paralyze me from just continuing to make all of them happen. Well Fear, your attempts to paralyze me with frustration and anxiety are over. What you, unfortunately, failed to realize is my desires have never been about me. My calling has always been much greater than me. These desires solely exist to inspire and reassure others that if I can do it, they can too! In turn, these individuals are destined to take this earth as we know it to the next level.

Fear, I believe you've had enough of my energy and it's time for me to offer my loved ones and the universe what it truly deserves. I accept that the balancing act will be a challenge and take discipline, but I will not accept that it's impossible. I have to be honest. When I made the commitment to write my story, I was afraid. I was ecstatic about the opportunity to participate in a project that empowers others to be the best version of themselves, as well as serve as a co-author in the same book as my mother-in-law, Alesha Salahuddin, and friend Latiera Streeter. I've always been interested in writing a book and started reading self-help books in high school. I actually remember riding in the car listening to Dr. Phil's Self Matters on CD. Despite my interest, I was afraid. I knew this journey would cause me to put myself in a certain light before I was ready. I believe people who have arrived should be authors, not me; not while I'm still writing my story. I have so much to share, but I need to wait until I get my life fully in order so I can be an inspiration, as opposed to making a commitment such as this one prematurely. My reputation means a lot to me, and if I'm going to write a book, I want to do it right and exceed the expectation as opposed to being underwhelming. So Fear, you will not have my process.

Signed,
Carla Ricks

YOU ARE HEADED
FOR GREATER,
STOP ALLOWING
FEAR TO STOP YOU

Dear Fear,
You Can't Have My Validation

You see, fear has a subtle way of appearing in our lives. It's intertwined within our personal beliefs about the world and ourselves, which makes it difficult for us to identify fear as the culprit to emotions such as anger, agitation, sadness, and anxiety. Majority of the time we relate the emotions to a person or situation when in actuality, fear is the root of what we're feeling. Fear personally appears in my life when unexpected circumstances conflict with my personal expectations or plans. I believe I've learned to live with fear by understanding fear's inception in my life and identifying fear for what it is when it attempts to reappear in my life today.

FEAR'S INCEPTION

Fear made its inception at an early age through the art of comparison. It constantly reminded me of everything I wasn't versus what I wanted to be. You see, for me, there are 4 things that make up my core: commitment, selflessness, consistency, and success. Fear found a way to attack each of these things using the people I loved and admired the most...my family.

My Dad

My dad is the oldest of five children and comes from a modest background. He is a retired U.S. Army Colonel and a big picture thinker. He's held multiple leadership positions throughout his career and is known for his ability to bring the right people together to complete tasks. He's very disciplined and also a health nut. He goes to bed early, wakes up early, starts his morning with a green smoothie, and works out a minimum of 6 days a week. My dad is involved in church and community, great at public speaking, taught me everything I know about money management, and loves his family. All of these characteristics inspire me to be disciplined and do what needs to be done even when I don't feel like it. His lifestyle inspires me to know anything and everything is possible with commitment and consistency.

My Mom

My mom is an only child and is literally the epitome of a PERFECT, working well-rounded mother. She has managed to keep an impeccably clean house, serve as a military wife, raise two girls, and continuously progress in her career. SHE DOES IT ALL! She cares about people and lives with a servant's heart. She greets everyone with whom she comes into contact with the same warm smile and exciting reverence of their sheer presence regardless of their status, age, or color. She loves my sister and me more than anything on this earth, including herself. She lives by the philosophy of helping others when they need it most. That love and selflessness inspires me. It inspires me to share it with others and do more than I think is possible because I've seen it done.

My Sister

Wow! My sister, Teresa. Where do I begin? Teresa is the first-born child that every parent wants. She is articulate, caring, ambitious, responsible, beautiful, and the list goes on. Teresa was very popular while growing up, but never carried a stuck up spirit that might usually accompany that level of status. Teresa typically doesn't have trouble with articulating her true opinion on a subject matter. She's vocal with her perspective, and 9 times out of 10 is usually right. Today, she has a small circle of friends and is extremely committed to giving her absolute best to them and family at all times. She makes being a working mother look easy. She wakes up on time, works out consistently, meal preps and eats healthy, manages multiple after-school activities for children, and is a self-motivated lifelong learner. Needless to say, she was an amazing person to look up to and continues to influence the standard for my personal blueprint of success.

THEN THERE WAS ME...

While growing up, my room was never clean on a consistent basis. I couldn't vacuum in straight lines, everything I did took twice the amount of energy. I didn't want to carry a purse or take time to get ready like my sister and mom, had a scatterbrained way of coming to conclusions, and despised arts and crafts. Compare this to a family full of commitment, consistency, selflessness, and success, and it was a recipe for my own inner disaster. I constantly compared my weaknesses to their strengths, and I became very unhappy with what I brought to the family. In my eyes, they were all masters of so many things, and then there was me. Fear convinced me that there would never be enough room for me to stand out, make a difference, be profound, or be relevant. No matter how much I made the family laugh or did things to make them smile, in my mind, anything I did would never be good enough for their level. My love and admiration for my family transitioned into insecurity and fear of irrelevance. By the time I started school, fear had made its inception into my life and it was my responsibility to make sure nobody found out the truth. Nobody could see how irrelevant I was. I had to prove to myself, and the rest of the world, that I was worthy of existing. And so the journey began.

The Journey of Perfection

Of course, as a child, I didn't notice fear had intercepted my life. At the time, I just believed it to be a reality. I felt like the odd one (and the least accomplished), so I put unnecessary pressures on myself to not just be good but to be great. If I was going to do something, it had to exceed the expectation and be done with a spirit of excellence. While growing up, I attributed these desires solely to being ambitious and wanting to get the most that life has to offer. It wasn't until reflecting as an adult, that I realized the amount of self-induced anxiety that came along with achieving large or small goals wasn't the norm. I didn't feel complete or comfortable with pulling the trigger on plans with anything I was unsure of without overthinking or talking things out with someone I trusted. I was able to learn that when anxiety and overwhelm shows itself, it's usually rooted back to that fear of me feeling the need to prove my worthiness and relevance to myself or others.

Living with Fear

At the time, I was sitting in the Dear Fear 2 book signing supporting Big Sisters Ashley Little and Shani Farmer when I made the decision to be part of Dear Fear. In this season, I was in an overwhelming space in life. I was in the process of settling into a new home, interviewing for new jobs after finding out my job would be transitioning across the country, redefining my identity as a wife and mother, and dealing with unexpected family illness. While all of these life happenings were not negative, they were extremely stressful because of the control I wanted but didn't have. Despite receiving the release I needed at the book signing after hearing snippets from each of the author's stories, fear tried to deter me from participating in Vol. 3 through my own thoughts. *I don't have time for this right now. I don't have a deep story to tell. I don't even like writing. I like the idea of the Dear Fear project, but I don't want to associate my name by being random with something I didn't strategically seek. You aren't going to be able to be consistent enough to complete this on top of your current commitments.* So many thoughts arose, and the pressure of not letting anyone down overwhelmed me.

But I took action! And that's what I want for you. Stop allowing fear to overwhelm you, keep you anxious and hold you back from taking necessary action in your life. See the fear, feel the fear, and still do it afraid.

I've learned to live fearlessly by understanding its purpose and accepting life as a journey, as opposed to a destination. Fear wants me to be overconsumed with trying to figure out how I messed up, or how I can fix situations that don't align with my expectations instead of accepting people for who they are. It wants me to be too overwhelmed to see life events as opportunities to stretch me out of my comfort zone, ultimately preparing me to fulfill my hearts desires and life purpose.

I still overthink; however, I have learned to recognize my thoughts as they come and re-channel my hesitations or fears to action. I spend less mental energy on what could happen or why, and more action on what I have the ability to control.

Below are a few things that help or have helped me to stay true to my purpose despite the appearance of fear:

1. **Pause and pray.**

2. **Cry.** Let out all the toxins and emotions through tears before action.

3. **Journal.** Especially if it deals with addressing a person. Journaling helps to get all of my rude comments and irrational emotions out the way before a conversation.

4. **Rising Strong by Brene Brown**

5. **Ask for help from a strong, trustworthy, inspiring circle of family and friends.**

1. **How are you able to identify fear in your life?**

_____

_____

_____

_____

_____

2. **What thoughts or techniques will you use to redirect fear the next time you notice it appearing in your life?**

_____

_____

_____

_____

_____

WHEN, IS NOW

ALIGNMENT IS BETTER THAN ACCEPTANCE

Bio

Carla Ricks is a native of Fayetteville, NC and a proud alumnus of North Carolina A&T State University where she majored in Agriculture Education with a concentration in Communications. Carla served as Miss North Carolina A&T 2010-2011 and was featured in Ebony Magazine's HBCU Campus Queens edition. During that time, Carla was instrumental in the planning and execution of Black Shadow's Day, a community service event designed for coaching, teaching, and mentoring high school students. Carla was also initiated into the Alpha Mu Chapter of Delta Sigma Theta Sorority, Incorporated.

Upon graduating college, Carla took an internship with the Volvo Group North American Headquarters in Greensboro, NC and worked her way up supporting various executive leadership and marketing teams throughout the organization. In June 2015, Carla relocated her talents to Washington, DC and served as a staffing consultant for Randstad before transitioning to the National FFA Organization as executive support to the Board of Directors and Advocacy and Government Relations division. In this role, Carla worked with legislative officials, the United States Department of Agriculture, and National FFA affiliates to help raise the profile of the Next Generation of Agriculture.

Carla finds motivation and joy in connecting with people from different environments, backgrounds, cultures, and perspectives. She understands and promotes the value of mentorship. Carla attributes all of her success to God and the people that have intentionally been placed in her life as her support system.

Carla currently serves as an Operations Specialist for the JP Morgan Institute in Washington, DC and resides in Upper Marlboro, MD with her husband Jason, son Caleb, and dog Bentley.

IF IT'S NOT IN ALIGNMENT, IT CAN'T BE APART OF YOUR ASSIGNMENT

SURRENDER TO
THE PROCESS

Dara Jones

Dear Fear,

You thought you had me, didn't you? You tried to drown me. You led me to believe that I was a failure. You told me that I had disappointed everyone I loved. You said that my dreams would take so much longer to attain that I might as well just give them up. You used my reluctance to ask for help as a prison. For once in my life, you were able to use the opinions of others to beat me down, and you did it so well. I've always been afraid of failure, so this season of my life was the perfect opportunity for you to slide in and wreak havoc.

Oh, but the God I serve! He had his hand on me, even when I was unable to verbally ask for help. He used my family and friends to reach down and pull me up from the darkness. He reminded me that you, Fear, have no place in my life. My faith is too great. You have no authority. He won't allow you to take me out because my story is someone else's lifeline. I am living proof that situations are temporary and that joy comes in the morning. Now that the morning has come, I'm telling my story for those who haven't made it to morning just yet.

Triumphantly,
Dara Jones

EVERYONE WON'T UNDERSTAND THE JOURNEY... GO ANYWAYS

Dear Fear,
You Can't Have My Light

I've known that I wanted to be a mother since I was 10 years old. Crazy, right? Through the eyes of a child, I watched the way my mother cared for my two siblings and myself and knew that I wanted to give the same nurturing and love to my own children. I had no idea that sometimes my mother went without eating so that we could. My village was so amazing, that until I was a teenager, I was blind to the fact that my mother struggled to take care of us. She did her job so well, that we only focused on the things we had, not the things we were lacking. Though my mother is still the strongest woman I know and my admiration knows no bounds, I vowed to make the *right* choices. The choices that would put me ahead in life, so I would never have to worry about struggling. I was HER.

You know her. In fact, if you're not her, you depend on her. She looks perfect from the outside. She is smart, makes the best choices, ignores peer pressure, and is a great role model; model daughter, sister, friend, Christian. She rescues, teaches, advises, sponsors, loves, protects, gives until she has nothing left. She does it all with a smile, outwardly looking like she needs nothing, so those around her never ask what she needs, and she never asks for help because ***who is left to ask when everyone needs you?***

I had my life all mapped out. I would go to school, get straight As, earn a scholarship to the college of my choice, graduate at the top of my class both undergrad and law school, meet my husband while in college, get married soon after graduation, buy a house, and start a family. My amazing, praying grandmother, who also happened to be an educator, worked with me before I was school age so I was already ahead of most of my classmates once I started school. School was a breeze, so I got the As, attended gifted programs and earned scholarships easily. My plan was working so far; I was ready. I went to college, and at first, things were going great, but then life happened. The loss of my grandmother left me bruised, broken and feeling as though God had snatched back the anchor to not only my life but the lives of so many of my family members. Though I was surrounded by friends, I felt alone. Between the devastating loss and my debilitating insomnia, I couldn't keep up with my grades. Sometimes I would go 48 consecutive hours without sleep. My tired body and frayed emotions left me unable to function. As you can imagine, my plan began to unravel right before my tired eyes. I couldn't maintain the one thing I was good at. I felt like a failure. I didn't know what my next move would be, but I knew I had to move. So, I prayed hard. Now, anyone who knows me knows that 1) I hate to get dirty, and 2) I'm not a fan of manual labor. But when taking my brother to take the Armed Services Vocational Aptitude Battery (ASVAB) test turned into me scoring an 86 on my first try, I thought surely my prayers were answered and I was supposed to join the service. And because I never second-guessed the decision, I knew it had to be divine intervention. Even my recruiter expected me to change my mind before it was time to sign on the dotted line. I couldn't allow myself to keep wasting money and adding to my student loans. I didn't want to disappoint my parents or have to rely on them while I figured my life out, so I enlisted in the Army.

I excelled in the Army. I'm a pretty structured person by nature, and there isn't much that phases me. It was, by far, the easiest job I've ever had. My only complaint was that sometimes we unnecessarily did things the hard way rather than the smart way. After six years (and plenty of wear and tear on my body), I left the Army with all of the invaluable lessons, knowledge, and friendships that I gained over the years. The Army afforded me the opportunity to go to school for free, so I immediately jumped right back into school full-time. I was determined to do well. I had to finish something. *I had to make up for failing before.*

I was flourishing, I mean knocking it out of the park. I was excelling in school and at my sought-after internship, in a loving relationship, swooping in and saving everyone in need, lending money, giving advice, budgeting exceptionally, and taking perfect pictures for the Gram (Instagram, for those of you who may not know) and Facebook. SHE was back and WE were great. **I was dancing happily around the edge of the pool.**

As I prepared for graduation in December 2017, I was on top of the world. Life was great. But on December 22nd, when I found out I was pregnant (only days after graduation), life as I knew it began to spiral out of control. It might sound kind of crazy, and this might be the first and only time I admit it, but when I found out I was pregnant with my daughter I went through the five stages of grief. **I was pushed into the pool.** Actually, if we're being real, I have to take ownership. I jumped; no, I did a cannonball into the pool. I knew better. I knew my actions didn't align with my beliefs or my master plan. My thoughts consumed me as I began to inwardly berate myself. *You just graduated a week ago and start graduate school next month. What are you going to do with a baby? Your parents are going to be so disappointed. You* *waited 31 years just to become a statistic. You bought the dream that was sold to you. You believed the promises of marriage and a future. What will the people that look up to you think? What will the people at CHURCH think?* Because let's be honest, church folks are some of the most judgemental folks we know. They'll tell you to forgive in one breath and judge you in the next. Ultimately, at the end of the day, this was my loudest thought: *Will he even stay? Either way, you're going to have to struggle. Just...like...your... mother.*

I had based my entire life on learning from the mistakes of others. I saw what they did, worked through the reasoning in my head, figured what they could have done differently, and shaped my own guideline based on the lesson. It was easy, right? Logical even. Just don't do what they did. But I had. I allowed a place I know I should not have been to become my comfort zone. Where I used to rest in the Lord, I began to rest in a man. My prayer life suffered, and I began to skip church. He became the center of my world. And my world turned in a slow yet sweet rotation with him, and I loved every minute on the precipice of everything that didn't align with my beliefs. But quite suddenly and without any real explanation, our relationship ended and my world no longer turned, it tilted.

Imagine starting the new year single, pregnant, depressed, and ashamed. I had to deal with all of the normal symptoms of pregnancy along with heartbreak. **I was treading water.** The times that I wasn't physically exhausted, I used life to stay busy. My daughter's father and I were on civil terms, and he did a great job of supporting me throughout the pregnancy. We hired a doula, went to appointments, and even found someone to do a 4-D ultrasound. I dove head first into school, volunteered, went to birthing classes, and gave all that I could at work. I did anything to keep my mind off my situation. And by *situation*, I don't mean pregnancy. *I* was the situation. I was afraid to deal with ME. I was afraid to ask myself the hard questions. Can you relate? Have you ever been afraid to get still because you would only be sitting with YOURSELF in the room?

Between my birth education classes, my doulas, and Ina May's Guide to Childbirth, I was ready; or so I thought. I was going natural but prepared for every scenario. A c-section was my last, last resort. Our bags were packed, I had my birth plan mapped out, and my doula was on call. After a few false starts and a week past my due date, I finally went into labor. Everything started out pretty simply. I handled the contractions throughout the night like a pro, but everything changed the next day. The pain started to rest in my back and became increasingly more intense irritating an old Army injury. Suddenly, I could barely catch my breath. My doula was coaching me through every seemingly endless contraction. As much as I was against the idea of drugs, I asked for an i.v. pain reliever, which was supposed to help with pain for a 2-3 hour span but it got to the point that it wasn't enough. The pain was so excruciating that I finally asked for an epidural. At this point, I was about 9 cm dilated and my cervix was swelling, so they put me in a new position to combat the swelling. My doctor was pleased with the idea of the epidural because he seemed to think it would relax me enough to let me rest and save energy for pushing. It took everything in me to hold on until the anesthesiologist arrived, but I told myself that I could hold on and that everything would improve once I got the epidural. My doula was so phenomenal. I think she could tell I was at my breaking point, so she never left my side. Everyone in the room ceased to exist but me and her. You should have seen the look of relief on my face when the anesthesiologist walked in the door. He did the procedure and gave me instructions about how everything worked. He said my legs would feel numb and that I could press a button when I needed more medicine. Too easy, right? Except the relief never came. The epidural didn't work. I pushed past all of that pain for 20+ hours. I got to 9 cm dilated. The pain was supposed to go away, but it never did. I couldn't do it. I had been at 9 cm for hours and the pain was unbearable, so I reluctantly opted for a c-section.

The moment they put the spinal tap in to numb me for surgery, my body instantly relaxed. I wanted to go to sleep more than anything. I had been in labor for 24 hours at that point, and my body was exhausted. The procedure was relatively short, and it wasn't long before I heard my daughter's first cry. You know how people are like, *I instantly fell in love as soon as I saw my baby's face.* Didn't happen...at least not for me. I saw her and thought, *Awww. Can I go to sleep now?*

The few days in the hospital were a blur. Baby girl had decided to bless us with her presence on Labor Day weekend, which I only realized was a problem when I couldn't get the medication I needed once I got home. I spent two whole days without medication, and if you've ever had a c-section or major surgery you can imagine how terrible it was. The pain was awful, and to add to that, my milk had come in but I was engorged. So there I was, in pain from my incision and engorged breasts with bloody cracked nipples, and a newborn. I couldn't feed her because it hurt and my breasts were too engorged. I felt terrible. My body was made for this. It should come naturally. I couldn't even feed my baby. I was only a few days in, and I was already messing everything up. My best friend and mother literally had to milk me like a cow, and nothing really worked until I was able to get pain medication. Once the meds kicked in, my body relaxed and I was finally able to maintain a sense of normalcy.

My daughter's father stayed for the weekend but had to return to school a few hours away, so my mom would go to work during the day and stay with us at night. My grandfather had also been sick for a while, and my mom was splitting her time between making sure we were ok and trying to do the same for him. I felt so overwhelmed. I was exhausted from her nightly feedings, still in pain from my incision, having issues with breastfeeding, and feeling like nothing I did was right. My incision didn't allow me to sleep comfortably in my bed, so I was on the couch. My daughter and I would sit there during the day and my thoughts would get the best of me. *Life as you know it is over. You'll never be able to do the things you wanted to do now. You're stuck here with a baby and he gets to go back to his old life. How on earth are you going to juggle graduate school with her? All she does is cry. Everyone is busy living their lives. How dare you think of inconveniencing them with your weakness?* The more I thought, the further I sank. It felt like the walls were closing in on me. **I was drowning.** I was alone in the deepest, darkest depths of my own consciousness, feeling as though I sank to the bottom of the ocean with no light in sight. I couldn't see past my pain. I would cry every day, multiple times a day. Sometimes my daughter and I would cry together. I would burst into tears mid-sentence in a conversation, sometimes not even knowing the cause of my tears. By the time my mom got home from work, all I could do was hand her over.

Two weeks after my daughter's birth, my grandfather passed. Of course, I was still dealing with hormones so every emotion was heightened. It broke me. My friends and family were checking on me pretty regularly, but to be honest I just wanted my mommy.

I would tell them that I was tired, but I was ok. I didn't want to burden them with what I felt was my responsibility. I made the mess, and I had to deal with it. I felt like it was selfish to need my mother while she was mourning the death of her father, so I put on a brave face and tried not to take too much of her time. She was dealing with enough, but I was sinking further into the depths. Every now and then my daughter would do something like smile in her sleep, and that would help reel me back in for a little while, but there were times when I thought, *death would be so much easier than this.*

That was the turning point for me. I knew I had to ask for help. I knew that my thoughts weren't normal, and in hindsight, I can identify them as postpartum depression. I prayed and asked God to help me. And just like the faithful, amazing God he has always been, he sent my support system to swoop in and save me. They threw me a life preserver and I am forever grateful for them. **They snatched my nearly limp body from the depths**. That first breath of air was exhilarating. I could see and hear clearly for the first time in weeks. No longer were my eyes masked in darkness. They called me, came and sat with me during the day, took my daughter for a few hours so I could nap, brought me food, went to my grandfather's funeral with me; anything I needed, they were right there. The more I asked for help, the better I felt. We went and stayed with my parents for a few weeks. Just knowing that they would be home with me after work was comforting. I still had low days, but I was coping better with the difficult moments. My support system would rejoice with me on the days that I would only cry once. That may sound silly, but for me, it was a serious improvement. Even now I have days that I have to give myself a pep talk or ask my mom to watch my daughter while I take a nap. It's a continual process that is constantly changing.

I want you to know that it's ok to not be perfect. It's ok to ask for help, it's not a weakness. It takes a strong person to identify the need and put their insecurities aside. Your support system is waiting for you to say the word, just like mine was. And if you don't have one, create one. Pray for God to place the right people in your life. Not meeting the expectations you set for yourself doesn't make you a failure. Life is fluid, and things won't always work out the way we plan, but we have to trust God's plan for our lives. Trust that he knows what's best for us, and believe that he has our best interest in mind. I want every woman who has gone through something similar to know that they're not alone and morning will come. No, morning is HERE! You are standing in your morning now. Fear couldn't take my light, and it won't take yours either. Press through this hard season of your life to get to the joy on the other side.

1. **Who is your support system?**

_____

_____

_____

_____

_____

2. **What are some techniques you use to combat depression?**

_____

_____

_____

_____

_____

YOU ARE MORE
POWERFUL THAN
YOU COULD EVER
IMAGINE

Bio

Dara Jones is a Human Resource professional, Army veteran, and the Director of Finance for Women's CEO Alliance. She has a Bachelor's degree in Business Administration with a concentration in Human Resource Management from Troy University and is an active member of SHRM. She is a personal assistant to her daughter, Kennedy, whose demands currently come in the form of cries. They reside in Dothan, AL.

STOP CHOOSING TO
GIVE YOUR POWER
AWAY

BE WISE ENOUGH TO
SEE THE PURPOSE IN
EVERYTHING

Aprill Joy

Dear Fear,

You captivated my mind releasing energy that was toxic to my character. Many times you left me unable to breathe, & the more I inhaled nothing that felt like life came out. Fear, you were the snake of my deepest disappointment. You snuck up on me every chance you got to scare me out my purpose.

You took a bite out of my arm and left the poisonous venom to captivate my body leaving me sweaty...continuing to leave me breathless. And when I'd attempt to find my voice to call you out as the liar you are, my voice would become shaky, my airway would close up quickly leaving me paralyzed with no hope of living. You constantly made me question myself. You continuously left me wondering if I was good enough and if I was living in the fullness of my purpose.

You were everywhere I went. The car, class, around my kids, in the courtroom. Many days you smelled so nice, enticing me, leaving me comfortable in your arms. But I realized fear, that your whispers, your choking, your belittling didn't line up to the will of God. You may have held me, but you couldn't keep me. Fear your venom no longer has me bound, I activated my antidote of faith. I'm no longer hypnotized with worry and unbelief. You tried it when you came for me. You apparently don't know who I am...so let me tell you. I am God's child. In fact, I'm His favorite. He favors me. His arms comfort me. I am no longer afraid of you. I am breathing. I am living. I am enough. Bump that, I'm MORE than enough.

I..am Aprill Joy. And YOU fear, can have several seats.

Signed,
Aprill Joy

FAILURE IS
NECESSARY FOR
SUCCESS

FEAR HAS NO
POWER OVER
YOUR LIFE

Dear Fear,
I am April Joy

I remember being 4 months pregnant with my planned last baby. I was so excited, yet fearful of what people would say about me. Interesting right? Here I am, 30 years old AND married. A grown woman that handled her business...yet I was afraid of what others would think. I called my husband to tell him the news, and he was so very excited, but I wasn't. And while he was rejoicing, thoughts flooded my mind shifting my focus from excitement to what the heck am I doing.

Here's why. Life for my marriage hadn't been a crystal stair. There were things that had gone undiscussed and unhealed before we jumped into expanding our family. If I had to be completely honest with myself, I was upset that I had spent our entire savings on keeping our family afloat for 10 years. Not to mention using my money that should have gone to my education, to open up a barbershop for us, just for my husband to close it within a few months. So there was that. And if I'm continuing on this honest journey with you, then I must share that I was also afraid of being a single mom of three if he left me a**gain** when something NEW caught his eye. (Yes you read that right) But I couldn't let that worry me. We were married, we were working, God was in it, and I believed I wouldn't go through any of that nonsense again. After all, I had my husband's word. He looked me in the eye and said, "I'm never going to hurt you again, and our family will be a testimony for other young couples ready to throw in the towel." I was ready and assured that this time was different.

99

Now I'm sitting here looking at my stomach, feeling flutters and planning a pregnancy announcement shoot. I think I'm ready to introduce the world to my unborn. On March 25th, I posted a picture with my family captioned, "There is no better way to bring in my 30th birthday. Jones Family Party of 5 Coming Fall 2017." A sigh of relief dropped to the pit of my stomach, however I noticed a change in my husband. The excitement my husband first showed was no longer there. How was he not excited to announce our planned child? Why was he agitated at the shoot? What changed? I'm the pregnant one. I had felt this feeling before. It felt way too familiar. I know you're wondering what I'm talking about. Ladies, it's that gut feeling that you feel when you know something is wrong, but you don't want to say too much because you don't want to cause an argument.

Or the thought that you may just be emotional and tripping, and if you say something it might result in that one dreadful sentence: I want a divorce. That was my life. I was afraid to rock the boat, afraid to ask too many questions because my real fear was the dreadful "d" word: divorce.

No wife should have to go through those mixed thoughts. Honestly, those are the thoughts that jumped up and down on my heart every six months for the years. Yes, every six months for the past few years, my husband would want out of the marriage. That was where my anxiety came from with our 3rd child. This is something I never thought I would share, but here we go.

I tried not to give him any reason to feel that way. I was working two jobs and was also a full-time student. He was a stay-at-home father and took really good care of the children. Not to mention, I loved everything about this man. He was my high school sweetheart and he was the man I gave my virginity to.

He was my forever, the one God told me that I would be doing ministry with. He was the one who would father all 5 of my kids, two whom which were not conceived. We both saw these visions. He was all I knew and I would have done anything for him. So I couldn't understand why he wanted out.

We wanted a house. My family built us one. We needed a vehicle, so my family ensured we had it. I didn't understand what more I had to do to prove that I was holding us down. I wanted to make sure I put us in a better position so he could further his dreams. I didn't realize, through the process, that I was compromising my identity. He would often say, "Go make friends, go chase your dream." But the reality was, my dream was to help him chase his, to be a good wife and loving mother. I didn't know anything other than that. Why couldn't that just be enough?

As you can see, I've always asked myself questions. I always second guessed my ability to make choices. He was the head, and I was the tail. All I wanted was my family; nothing more, nothing less. So now I'm sitting here 5 months pregnant with overwhelming mixed feelings. *When will it be my time to become what I see in myself? I mean, how can I see the value in myself that everyone else sees? When will enough be enough, and when will I really stand firm on not allowing someone who leaves to keep coming back? When am I going to stop the cycle?*

April 2017 came, and he started his new job. I was excited that I could finally take a break from working and just be a mother and wife. I needed a break! But what I wasn't expecting was the break that was on its way. Almost one month after announcing our pregnancy to the world, he came to me with those dreadful words.

I want a divorce.

My mind is flooded with thoughts. *Divorce? After begging me for another child?* Fear was winning, and I was losing everything; my mind, my joy, my voice, my heart, my essence. All I could do was pray that God would change his mind. I remember hearing God say this was different. As he prepared to move out, I was looking at my two children wondering, *how do I tell them **AGAIN** that their dad is moving out? How am I going to face the world?* Let's be honest, this has happened before, so it shouldn't come as a surprise. But I wanted to make sure he was sure because this time was different. I had a child in my stomach.

See, this is the moment I had to change my mindset. I had to change my mindset for myself first, but then also for my three babies. My children needed to see me in a better place. If I didn't owe them anything else, I owed them an opportunity at a healthy life. I had to come to the realization of who Aprill Joy was. As a good woman, you should never question if you are good enough. You will never be good enough for the wrong person. It was a hard pill to swallow because he wasn't just anyone, he was my forever. But that wasn't what he wanted. It should never be up to a man to see your value. If he wants to go, let him go, sis. Don't let someone control your mind to the point that you allow yourself to become the cycle. I should not have let someone choose time and time again to abandon me. As the months passed, I found myself searching for Aprill Joy. I found myself praying for Aprill Joy, and I found myself loving on her. She was a beautiful, loving, creative soul. She knew her worth and was ready to embark on this journey of new found love.

I slayed that pregnancy hunny! I worked my business and I took care of my children. I even covered my husband. Very few people knew that my husband left me, and I was confident in that. One month before I had my son, he was packing and moving out. I thought I would be hurt, I thought I would cry. I even thought I would have begged him to stay. However, this time was different. I held the door as his friends helped move the heavy items out. As the last item was moved, I sat and ate some cold watermelon. I have no idea why I was so calm. I guess I was tired of the inconsistency, or better yet, it was because God was doing a new thing and he was telling me to trust the process.

Now I'm holding my son, my everything. He was one of the three people that kept me focused. Soon after his birth, I was faced with yet another hurdle. After numerous doctor visits and uncontrollable puking, baby Kizer was admitted to the hospital. He had pyloric stenosis, meaning the muscle of the pylorus was thicker than normal making it hard for his food to pass through his stomach. He had to have surgery to fix the problem. I was emotionally hurt and still healing from my c-section, but I mustered up enough strength to sit in the hospital bed for three days with him. As I sat there holding him, wishing the pain away, I remember saying, "I'm going to trust the process. God, whatever you are doing I'm listening."

A few months passed and I received yet more shocking news. After a visit with their dad, my children came home and told me that they had met their step-mom and that she was going to have their baby sister in a month. All I could think was *wait a god darn minute.* See, this was a rumor that I was told. I asked him about it, but he denied it at the time. Our son was only 4 months old. I could not believe what I was hearing. But wait, he told our children before he told me. He introduced our kids to this woman that he denied. Ladies, all I could think was *what are you doing?* I would be lying if I told you I wasn't hurt. I think I was more hurt because that was the only thing he hadn't done to me. He had never fathered a child outside of our three. Mixed emotions ran through my head.

But God! God held me together. He allowed me to see myself. He wanted to show me that I was strong enough, and I was created just for this. As a younger woman, I always wanted to have a testimony. I felt like I had never gone through enough for my story to be considered a testimony. You better be careful of what you wish for because you just don't know what you will receive. Through me trusting the process, I found out that Aprill Joy is definitely one of a kind. I also realized that I have my own ministry in me, as each of us do. We are placed on this Earth for a reason, and sometimes our reason has to be discovered when we are at our lowest point.

Before, when I looked in the mirror, I saw myself as just his wife. Now, when I look in the mirror, I know that I am more than enough. I am joy. I am life. I am purpose. I am God's child. I am strong. I am resilient. I am confident. I am favored. I am Aprill Joy. I am one of the most sought-after photographers in the tri-state. I'm a mom that is doing the thang with three children. I'm a college graduate that will specialize in Elementary Education. I'm also working on a photo journal called "I do, I did: The Photo Journey to Becoming Aprill Joy."

These past two years I have grown and learned so much about myself. I have met so many people that have shared similar stories. I know my life is still being written by the author, but one thing is for sure, I will never allow anyone the opportunity to choose what's best for me again. So Fear, you thought you had my mind, but I know who I am, and whose I am.

1. When did you know your cycle of hurt was over?

_____

_____

_____

_____

_____

2. Can you love someone enough to let them go, if letting them go means letting you grow?

_____

_____

_____

_____

_____

Bio

April Joy is a successful photographer based in Dothan, Alabama. She is mother to three wonderful children: Kinson (10), Kaziah (8) and Kizer (1). She has a passion for youth education, and after a few obstacles, obtained her degree in Elementary Education from Troy University. Her photography business, Aprill Joy Photography, specializes in creative portraits. Aprill's journey is definitely not finished. She will be launching her first photo journal in the near future entitled *I do, I did: The Photo Journal to Becoming Aprill Joy* as well as a short film.

PUSH PAST YOUR PAIN

PUSH PAST
YOUR QUIT

Latiera Streeter

Dear Fear,

You've lurked long enough. No more penetrating my thoughts or seeping into my consciousness. Thank you for the times that you've saved my life and re-routed some of my bad decisions. However, the influence you've had over my life is no longer needed. This so-called relationship ends NOW. Not now...but RIGHT NOW! I've had enough of being my own obstacle, so I need you to move. In fact, I need to move out of the way. As long as I can remember, I've had high expectations. When I was younger, I wanted to keep up with the Jones', but didn't know how my mom, a single parent, would pay for it all; but we figured it out. As a teenager, you tried really hard to distract me from what God had already laid out in his blueprint for me. Haha, I made it to North Carolina Agricultural & Technical State University anyway. The expectations that were etched in my mind and flowed through my DNA were almost paralyzing. They stopped me dead in my tracks. Everyone said I would be okay, that what I accomplished was wonderful, and that I was amazing. But I felt like I hadn't done enough, it was never enough. I came to realize that I wasn't afraid of letting others down, I was afraid of letting myself down.

I made lists, wrote inspirational notes, searched for quotes, prayed, cried, hollered...and I was still afraid.

But no more. I have faced fear, and let me tell you she ain't pretty. She's a very unattractive version of me. I mean, she looks kind of like me, but a really pitiful version of me. Do you know why she looks like that?

111

Because she's scared of disappointing herself. I looked in the mirror and realized that what I'm really afraid of is ME. I wear my crown like a wreath of expectations. I've crowned myself in a cloak of perfection, well kind of. I'm not talking about that gorgeous shiny headpiece, though I proudly adorned one some years ago. I'm referring to the symbol of who we are. Some of us wear it boldly while others have it tucked away; buried so that others can't see it. Regardless, we all own a crown of responsibility and expectations; the crown of being a sister, brother, aunt, mentor, first in the family to go to college, survivor, woman, man and the list goes on.

I have huge expectations for myself. I want things done a certain way and I want, no I EXPECT certain outcomes. When things happen in accordance with my plan, I rejoice. But when they don't; hunny, I am devastated. You have a way of doing that to me. Of making me feel like I failed because things didn't go as planned. It traps me in a web of defeat, I let it consume me, and at times it has temporarily immobilized my being. Thank God, you tend to leave me alone and allow me to pull it together and re-route my original plan.

Fear, you will no longer hold me captive. I will do my best, give my best and I will honor the value therein. You will no longer tell me that not meeting my expectations is a failure. You will no longer win. I'm focused on the jewels that shine in my crown when it's heavy and weighs me down. You know, like when the sun hits it at just the right angle. That light, those gems...they represent effort, triumph, and victories. I will focus on those beams of light and raise my head. Chin up, Latiera. Listen, I think perfection is cool. I mean, who doesn't want all their ducks in a row? But perfection isn't always possible. I've learned to differentiate expectation from perfection.

I've embraced that expectation is less about meeting goals and more about a strong belief in something. So Fear, you keep the barometer of perfection. I don't need that anymore. I'll keep my beliefs and focus on the achievements I make every single day of my life. I'll keep striving, hoping and dreaming. Because there is power in letting go of things being everything I expected, and relishing in the successes along the way. There's a goal and a plan connected to everything I do. I will stumble when you try to trip me with "what ifs." But I'll dust myself off and keep on moving. I will pause when you block my path, but I will not be stopped. My personal expectations are not wrong; I will not apologize for them. Fear, I will not let you try to rationalize and barter with me to lower them, and then ultimately give up. For there is power in forward motion. This crown is heavy, bejeweled with more expectations than I can count. But it's cool, Fear. I've learned to embrace the beauty of imperfection.

Signed,
Latiera Streeter

PUSH PAST
YOUR GUILT

PUSH PAST
YOUR PAST

Dear Fear,
I Am Not My Crown

It scares me to admit this, and it scares me even more to share it with you, but I'm going to say it anyway: I am so afraid of not being good enough that I created a crown of expectations. This crown represented everything I was supposed to do and everything I was supposed to be; for myself, for my family and for the world. How can I be everything to the entire world? The crown became my measurement of success. Every time someone said, "Latiera is going to be...(fill in the blank, you name it they said it)," it added a jewel to the crown. I grew up in a small town, and we all knew each other, so people had A LOT to say about what I was going to do and who I was going to be. And each time someone expressed what I would be, the crown got heavier and heavier.

Listen, once I came to this realization I started doing research. I wondered *what's wrong with me, why I am like this?* I know I'm not the only one that goes to Google University when life seems unbalanced. Guess what? According to Web MD, there is a condition called atelophobia, which is the fear of not doing something right or the fear of not being good enough.

In other words, it's a fear of imperfection.

That condition seemed to describe me at the core, but after reading the definition, I had more questions that Web MD just couldn't answer. How did I come to relate with atelophobia, and where did it come from?

Have you ever become so future-oriented that you were presently absent? In my constant pursuit of "success", I realized that I wasn't enjoying my current victories. Since I can remember, I've always set lofty goals for myself. I would easily consider myself an ambitious person. I feel as if I've attempted to map out my entire life since I was in grade school. If you're anything like me, you've always known which college you wanted to go to, which profession you were going to enter, how many children you wanted...the list can go on forever. And my list does go on.

Yet, as life continues to unfold before your eyes and some of the benchmarks on your timeline go unchecked, you begin to doubt if they may ever happen. As adulthood set in, I started to wonder. *Why I am so pressed about the future? Am I too goal oriented? Is that even possible to be TOO goal oriented? Why are my expectations of myself so high? Are they too high?* Thoughts of imperfection clouded my judgment and crowded my mental space, but I knew it was time to dig a little deeper.

This crown that I wore was heavy because I made it that way. On the outside, it was beautiful, bedazzled and bejeweled. It smiled and it waved. It had the best friends and the best opportunities. But on the inside, this crown was broken, mentally jaded, and abused with thoughts of never being good enough. As I dug deeper, I began to take the crown apart so I could figure out its essence and discover the root of its existence. I realized that this crown didn't just appear. It was built. I built it. I molded it. I searched for the jewels. I covered it in gold. It was perfect for me...until it wasn't.

Designing the Crown

"She is the one who will do more than the others."

I can still hear my grandmother saying that phrase to people everywhere we went together. The "she" that my grandmother was talking about was me and the "others" were my siblings and cousins. I felt as if I was the "chosen one." I was unknowingly put on a pedestal. As long as I can remember, the one constant in my life has always been my grandparents, even after their deaths in the early 2000s. You couldn't tell me that I wasn't their favorite. They left a legacy for me to carry that I didn't even realize was so deeply rooted in who I am. So much that it scares me to even think about letting them down; even now, some 19 years later.

When they passed away, they secretly left me to take care of the family, or at least that's what I conceptualized. You see, the crown was being designed for me with the seeds being planted in me unintentionally.

Mommy was a young parent, not only young but a single parent with multiple jobs for most of my childhood. Being at my grandparents' house was second nature to me. Not having enough money to go on all the summer trips or pay for extra-curricular activities at Sunnyland Park and the PAL center didn't faze me because my grandmother always had a few dollars under the carpet, behind the door or under the left side of the mattress for me. I never missed a beat. I became accustomed to never missing a beat. My grandfather paraded me around like a princess. I would ride with him in his orange Ford pick-up truck to visit his friends, go to flea market and get the latest Pro Wings from Payless. We didn't have much, but they ensured that I had everything I could have ever wanted or needed. This lifestyle led me to believe that I needed to do the same thing for others when I grew up, especially my family. My family should never miss a beat. I would make sure of that. Spoken and unspoken expectations and responsibilities were engrained in me at a very young age. My crown of expectations and responsibilities was unconsciously designed for me by a family legacy woven into my being, blindly accepted before I could even realize the responsibility.

STREETER LEGACY. CROWN DESIGNED.

Pouring of the Mold

I was oblivious to not having my father present because my grandfather, MC, filled that void; and at times my step-fathers filled in too. I have such keen summer memories of getting dropped off at Church Street Station in Orlando, FL (the meeting spot) and running to my dad like he was my superhero. He taught me how to swim, bought me school clothes, and then it was time to go back home. But then, the superhero turned into super unreliable. The infrequent pop-ins of the Debutante father-daughter dance, and missing my high school graduation was a constant reminder that I wasn't a daddy's girl. Looking into the stands and searching for his face; well, maybe I just couldn't see him and he will have flowers for me like the other dads after graduation. No, he never showed. Honestly, the longing to be a daddy's girl would never come to fruition. And here came fear, and fear brought doubt, and doubt told me that I wasn't good enough. What was wrong with me? I was a pretty good child, didn't cause many problems, was the apple of my mom's eye, but I could never catch or keep the attention of my dad. Missed birthdays, unanswered calls, and broken promises were clear indicators that I wasn't enough. Doubt was right. As a young adult, I would often talk about my dad as if we were close. I boldly stated that he was an attorney and the first black Assistant State Attorney in my home county. Deep inside all of those accolades being shouted for daddy meant nothing when I was really yearning to boldly say, "Yep, I'm a daddy's girl!" The pressure and desire of being a daddy's girl would quickly come to a halt when I would hear, "Oh, Ricky has a daughter?"

It was at his 65th birthday, recently, that I realized that some of his closest friends and some of my family didn't even know I existed! Tears flowed for many years about the self-imposed expectation that I would one day be daddy's girl. And they still do. The pain is still there. And while we are working on having a solid relationship, the mold that was poured to form my crown reeks of never being good enough. Another jewel attached.

Mold. Poured.

Placement of the Crown

Vote for Laticra for Miss Mainland High School! Vote for Latiera for Miss Volusia County Teen! Vote for Latiera for Miss Freshman! Vote for Latiera for Miss Sophomore! The results came in – denied, I lost. At that moment, fear and doubt crept in with their whispers of "enough." I wasn't good enough, nice enough, pretty enough to hold those titles. Although I continued to smile on the outside, internally I was distraught. Did I really not have what it took to win a title and wear the crown? It started here; as I told you, the crown was this shiny unattainable object. I put the crown on a pedestal long before anyone else did. It always felt like it was just out of my reach. I entered the contests and ran the campaigns. I smiled until my face hurt and waved until my wrist was stiff. And still, I lost. With each loss, the pedestal felt farther from my reach. And each loss hurt. I couldn't figure out what I was doing wrong or what was wrong with me. I couldn't understand why I wasn't good enough to win.

As God worked on me and through me, eventually I realized that my purpose of serving in that "Queen" capacity was delayed not denied.

I always wanted to leave Florida and go away to college, so having the opportunity to attend North Carolina A&T was a dream. Although I earned Florida-based scholarships and my mom encouraged me to stay in-state, I followed my dreams and started on a new path. Living on campus, eating at the café, struggling to purchase books, and eating ramen noodles that my mom sent in my care packages definitely built character. It was a struggle to make ends meet, but I'm a Streeter, so I never missed a beat and made it work. My struggles were never publicized, and I made sure of that. I was very involved in extracurricular activities, worked on campus, worked a few hours at Gymboree on the weekends, modeled with one of the best modeling troupes, partied with the Greeks, and screamed "Aggie Pride" at all of the sporting events. Even on my summer breaks, I worked multiple jobs and secured summer internships, all to make sure my struggles wouldn't rear their head and be exposed to my friends.

I went to college expecting an *A Different World* experience, and for the most part that is what I had. College was refreshing because everyone was new to me and had no expectations. It was like a fresh start in some ways. I loved every minute of my college life and relish in the memories from the experience. But one thing I realized is that there was some extra baggage there. Apparently, when I packed my clothes, Winnie the Pooh pajamas and matching bedding to head off to Greensboro, North Carolina, I subconsciously packed those homegrown expectations. I brought them 546 miles away from home, and they became part of my college experience as well.

Little did I know, that after having a conversation with a classmate in the dormitory laundry room and reading about the story of Esther becoming a queen at bible study, that God would grant me the opportunity to serve in a capacity greater than I could have ever imagined. I solicited funds from my community and family, campaigned, the students voted, and I became the 70th Miss North Carolina Agricultural and Technical State University. At the end of coronation night, I sat back and reflected. I stared at that crown, and for a brief (and I do mean brief) moment I was at peace. As I looked at that crown on my head, those thoughts began to invade my mind. *How was I going to pull this off?* Imagine the crown of expectations I set for myself in addition to continuing the legacy of the role. I didn't come from money, I didn't have any money and I didn't know where or how I was going to represent my university without any money. At that time, I didn't even own a suit.

CROWN. PLACED.

Adjust the Crown.

Not only did I get a suit, but I earned my undergraduate degree and an MBA. Crown secured. I was right on track with checking off boxes on my life to-do list. Great news, right? Wrong. Somehow, those check marks caused the crown to slip. Why? I had two degrees, became a homeowner by the age of 30 and had a great job, but it wasn't enough. Being on track with my checklist, for some reason, was not a sign of success for me. After my MBA graduation party, when all the guests were gone, I exhaustedly sat down on my couch. My house was completely silent, and I was alone. The STILLNESS for many would be a sense of calm, but for me, it created a sense of panic. I was on track, but that wasn't enough. The atelophobia invaded my mind, breaking the silence as the questions flooded my soul. *What was next and how long was it going to take me to check the next box?*

And at that moment, I created a new list of expectations, adding weight to a crown that was just securing its place on my head. More jewels, more adjustments. Strangely enough, I found comfort in this, and I got back to work and became comfortable in seeking a new level of perfection. In the twinkling of an eye, my crown became so heavy that I thought it just might fall. A breast self-examination revealed a lump. The ultrasound confirmed the lump. The biopsy results read benign. Thank God! This was a wakeup call of God's grace. It was a reminder that things will not always go as planned, and when that happens, God has already prepared me and given me the strength to "Adjust my Crown."

At every stage, I added a jewel. My crown of perfectionism was so heavy that it trapped me in a web of defeat. The weight of it caused unnecessary stress, anxiety and sometimes even depression. I was tired…jaded, bruised. I came to the realization that I spend way too much time on perfecting simple tasks; things that, in the grand scheme of LIFE, don't really matter. I often drive myself and others crazy in the process. We all know someone who needs everything to be perfect…with work, at home, in relationships. I am that someone; a perfectionist with every aspect of my life. Often times things suffer in my pursuit of perfection. And the "thing" that suffers most…is ME.

I've learned that a perfectionistic outlook is no fun. I live in the future, meaning that the present is a risky situation where every mistake has enormous ramifications later. Everything is a perpetual threat, so I'm constantly scanning for worst-case scenarios, always trying to dodge any potential for error or criticism. My focus on the perfect result paralyzes my ability to focus on the steps necessary to reach my goals.

Listen, don't get me wrong, having high standards and working hard really does produce results. That's what is so insidious about trying to be perfect. When you're rewarded all your life for being thorough, detailed, and producing high-quality results, it doesn't merely become a habit — it becomes your identity. And that's what happened to me, it became my identity. Here are a few strategies that have helped me come to my senses.

1. **Re-evaluate My Standards** – Get real! Embrace the SMART (Specific, Measurable, Achievable, Relevant and Time-bound) goals concept by setting standards that are realistic and attainable. I stopped thinking that every time I adjusted my standards that it equated to lowering them.

2. **Give Myself Permission to Push Through Perfection** – Embrace that perfection is rarely possible, but that giving my best always is. When I set goals, I now focus more on the steps involved in reaching that goal, not just the end result. Being aware that obstacles are inevitable and being okay with that is part of the process.

3. **Don't Sweat the Small Stuff** – I have learned how to put challenges in perspective, reduce stress and anxiety through small daily changes, and focus more on enjoying the journey to achieving my goals.

Adjust the Crown. This saying has become so modernized, but what does it this really mean? You are constantly giving your best, working hard and trying hard, but still can't give yourself credit.

1. **In what way does your crown of imperfection show up in your life?**

_____

_____

_____

_____

_____

2. **What can you do today to release the weight of your crown and live your best life?**

_____

_____

_____

_____

_____

JOY IS HERE

EVERYBODY CAN'T GO WHERE GOD IS TAKING YOU

Bio

Latiera D. Streeter has over twelve years of accounting, compliance, internal controls, business operations, financial and strategic management experience. She is very passionate about developing sustainable solutions for a myriad of client-presented challenges. In addition to her creative approach to complex concepts and aptitude to analyze problems while challenging "the way it has always been done" approach, Latiera founded a mentoring program called Perspectives at her former accounting firm. The program's mission is to bridge the gap between entry-level employees and upper-level management.

Prior to joining her current management consulting firm, Latiera spent four years as an internal auditor where she provided guidance and direction for numerous clients utilizing her expertise in compliance and internal controls. While there, Latiera co-founded an Intergenerational business resource group. Latiera has been recognized by her employers and colleagues on many occasions for her outstanding performance.

Latiera holds a B.S. in Accounting from North Carolina Agricultural & Technical State University (NCA&T SU). While at NCA&T SU, she served as Miss North Carolina Agricultural and Technical State University 2004-2005 as well as Miss Junior 2003-2004. As Miss North Carolina A&T, Latiera was adamant about serving the students, making sure the university knew the real meaning of being a queen and leaving her personal dent in A&T's rich soil. Building a bridge between young girls and society and educating women of their self-worth was no stranger to Latiera. During her reign, she served as President of an organization called Ladies of Excellence, an organization that promotes business etiquette and professionalism amongst women on and off campus. In addition to presiding over Ladies of Excellence, Latiera spent countless hours volunteering and fostering relationships with the 4th and 5th-grade girls at Hampton Leadership Academy (Elementary School).

Latiera later received her MBA with a concentration in International Business from Howard University in 2014. Latiera uses her financial and business acumen, as well as her passion for helping others, by assuming various leadership positions in the community. She is the co-founder of Queen to Queen, Inc., an organization that fosters relationships among current and former queens of Historically Black Colleges and Universities (HBCUs) and supports the legacy of the HBCU queen. She is also an active member of Alpha Kappa Alpha, Sorority, Inc. where she formerly served as her chapter's Social and Welfare Committee Chairman and currently serves as the Rituals Chairman and a member of the North Atlantic Region's Hodegos Committee; an Audit Committee member of the Washington, DC National Pan-Hellenic Council; the former Treasurer and current Vice President of her discipleship group at Alfred Street Baptist Church and a member of the Golden Key International Honour Society.

Latiera continues to find inspiration in the anonymously written quote, "Care more than others think is wise, risk more than others think is safe, dream more than others think is practical and expect more than others think is possible." When not in the office, Latiera enjoys traveling, reading and shopping; but she is truly in her element when planning events and spending time with family and friends.

Pamela Knight

Dear Fear,

You cannot have my breakthrough. For so long, you made yourself a fixture in my life. You provided me with a false sense of security like you were my friend. We had a love/hate relationship. You constantly inserted yourself into my life, my thoughts, and my actions with the intent of deterring me from my purpose. Anytime I had an idea or a vision for myself, I allowed you to whisper doubting thoughts into my mind. You would attack my sense of confidence and make me question whether or not I had what it took to be who I am destined to be. At the same time, I embraced you because I felt that you were that voice in my head that was looking out for my well-being. It seemed as though you had my best interest at heart. As a result, I did not step out on faith or move when God instructed me to move. Therefore, I encountered situations and people in my life that made my path even more difficult than it needed to be. I am angry with myself because I allowed you to have that much influence over me. I hated you for making me feel that weak, like I had no control over my destiny. There were many sleepless nights and tears because I knew that there was something missing from my life, but I was stagnant. I was scared to reach for my dreams for fear of failure. I was so tired of feeling this way.

I finally woke up and recognized you for what you are. You are not and have never been, my friend. The season where I allowed you to have so much influence over my life is over. It's my turn, and I choose me. You can't have my mind, my body, my spirit, or my purpose because MY value has already been predetermined by God. With prayer and supplication, I will boldly walk into my full potential. So Fear, consider yourself bound with no means of escape. I know that I am strong because God did not create in me a spirit of fear.

Signed,
Pam

CONNECT WITH THOSE THAT CAN CALL FORTH YOUR SEEDS OF GREATNESS

ELEVATION REQUIRES SEPARATION FROM YOUR FEAR

Dear Fear, You Can't Have My Breakthrough

At the age of five, fear introduced itself to me when my parents announced that they were getting a divorce. Up until that point, I was in my own little bubble. I was now in unfamiliar territory and did not know what to expect. I was a daddy's girl. In my physical appearance, I looked just like my dad. Although my dad could be very stubborn with others, I rarely saw that side of him. He took me everywhere with him. I was considered to be his pride and joy. When the divorce occurred, I knew that things would never be the same. No more sitting in front of the television eating all the snacks and hearing my mother fuss because my appetite was spoiled. No more riding around in his car going to different places just because we felt like it. I knew that the quality time that we spent together would be limited. My parents made sure that I understood that it was not my fault and that I was loved very much by both parents. This is the type of environment in which I was raised.

However, I recognized that some of my peers that were going through the same thing were not as fortunate and struggled with adjusting. I decided that I wanted to help others with learning how to cope with difficult situations. At the age of 12 years old, I decided that I wanted to be a therapist.

I remember telling my mom that I was going to be a doctor with my own business. Being the supportive mom, she always told me that I could do anything I set my mind to do. So, I guess you could say that I received my vision early in life. I began to work toward that vision. As an adult, I now have a clear vision. My vision consists of creating an environment that takes the process of healing to another level; people being freed from mental bondage, trauma, spiritual distress, generational curses, etc. How many of you know that once you have recognized your purpose, it is only a matter of time before fear attempts to test you and deter you from your path? For those of you who know about fear, you know what I'm talking about. For those of you who don't know about fear, let me tell you about how fear operates.

Fear will mask itself as your friend. What do I mean by that? I'll use myself as an example. Fear positioned itself in my life where it could whisper words of doubt into my mind, cause confusion, and stop me from moving toward my vision. As I attempted to work toward my vision, fear presented itself in the form of some of my teachers and peers. Those teachers and peers tried to discourage me and challenge me in every direction. Even though fear utilized this as a way to make me feel defeated, my God was preparing me for something bigger. I learned some key lessons. First, I had to toughen up. I could not show any vulnerability or weakness. Second, my work and work ethic had to be ten times better than my peers. Last but not least, failure was not an option. These lessons provided me with success throughout my academic years and while building my business. However, fear is a trickster, more of a strategist. So when you challenge your fear to progress and move forward, fear comes at you in another way. You see, fear has the POSSIBILITY of fighting dirty and attacking you mentally, physically, and spiritually when it is challenged. Fear will issue its own challenge, and that's what it did for me.

One night, I received a call from my cousin that my dad had a stroke in his townhome in Connecticut. Upon arrival at the hospital, the doctor informed me that not only did my dad have a stroke, but he was also suffering from Stage IV Renal Disease and was refusing to be placed on dialysis. That same fear that was introduced to me years ago when my parents divorced was back, but now taking it to another level. There was a real possibility that I might lose my dad. Those of you who have older parents know what I mean; the stubbornness. I think my dad was more stubborn than the average.

However, I was faced with having to talk with my dad about whether or not he wanted to live or die. Let's be honest, what child wants to face the death of a parent? Due to being the only child, I did not have the luxury of burying my head in the sand and refusing to address the issue. So I slipped into therapy mode and had the discussion with my dad, knowing that he may say that he was tired of being sick and ready to die. Truth be told, I wanted to be selfish and say that he didn't have a choice because I was not prepared to possibly hear the words that he was ready to die. Luckily, that was not the case. However, things became worse.

Due to my dad's resistance to participating in physical therapy, the rehabilitation program wanted to discharge him, but he could not return home due to the fact that he was considered to be a fall risk. Therefore, it was time to talk to my dad about moving to Virginia. By this time, I was trying to see to all of his medical needs, run his household in Connecticut, run my business in Virginia, and maintain the rest of my life. Sounds like a lot, and it was. I was physically and mentally exhausted. So, I suggested to my dad that he move to Virginia where I could look after him better. Dad refused to move and struggled with understanding the reason he was unable to return home. He was miserable at the rehabilitation center, and I felt guilty. Although I knew that I had no choice but to keep him in the rehabilitation center for his safety, I felt guilty whenever I talked to him. My dad was so independent. I remember my dad being such a strong man and full of life. He no longer resembled that strong man that I knew when I was younger. It pained me to see how fragile he was and how forgetful he was becoming. Fear crept into my mind and told me that I was failing him. Earlier in the chapter, I mentioned that I developed the mentality that failure was not an option. Well, fear threw that back into my face.

Here I am, a person whom people come to for assistance with their healing and for help with coping with significant life stressors, and I felt like I was failing at taking care of one of the most important people in my life. Although I was doing all that I could possibly do from Virginia, it did not seem to be enough. When my dad realized that he would not be able to return home, he agreed to move to Virginia. While this was a relief because I would be able to keep an eye on him and monitor his health, it placed even more pressure on me. At this point, I had to sell his home, get rid of his furniture, close bank accounts, transfer insurance, and go back and forth to court due to a *shady* rehabilitation center and their actions. For me, this was a dark place and time. This is where fear utilized my mentality of being tough against me. I had plenty of friends to talk to and lean on, but I didn't because I was operating under the notion that I should be able to handle it. I became great at putting on a mask so no one knew how overwhelmed I was at the time. I was not eating or sleeping. I had no energy to do anything. At night, I would just lay in bed and cry myself to sleep. I was so stressed to the point that I began experiencing chest pains. It was at that point, I knew I had to do something different. First, I identified a friend to lean on at the time. I would call her to just vent about it all; a way to release the feelings on the inside. Her role was to just...LISTEN. The key is to RELEASE all of the emotions that you are stuffing on the inside. If not, it will start to affect you physically. Second, I put myself on a self-care plan. You cannot take care of anyone else if you cannot take care of yourself. Being selfish is given such a negative connotation, but being selfish is sometimes necessary. Third, it is okay to ask for help. This is not considered to be a weakness but a sign of strength. We ALL need help at some point in time...especially those who are in the role of helping others. Last, but not least, pray without ceasing. There were times when I prayed, I cried, and felt alone. I feared that God was not hearing me or answering my prayers, so I became angry with Him.

Now, I know that we have been taught not to question God or become angry with God. This is my thought process on that ideology. If we call ourselves being in a relationship with God, then why is this an issue? Do you really think that God cannot handle your anger? If you cannot acknowledge your feelings, then how can you address the feelings that may hinder you from growing closer to God? This is what fear wants...to have you question your relationship with God, your purpose, and God's potential for your life. Face your fears, acknowledge your feelings, and continue to build your relationship with God.

In the end, my dad moved to Virginia. I was so grateful that I had the opportunity to spend more time with him. He began to regain his strength and laugh again. Unfortunately, my dad passed away five months after moving to Virginia. In reflecting on this time in my life, I was able to recognize that fear used my dad's final transition to test my strength, confidence, knowledge, purpose, and faith. I couldn't see past my fears.

Although I was physically present, I was not mentally present or focused. Because if I was mentally present, I would have recognized my own brokenness and my resistance to surrendering and being vulnerable in my situation. As tough as my dad's final transition was for me, I learned an invaluable lesson. You cannot half step your way through your healing and expect to come out whole. I cannot engage others and take them to another level in their healing process if I'm unwilling to go on the journey myself. Once I was able to recognize fear in my life, I called it out. I challenged myself to put fear in its place and focused on my healing and rebuilding my life. My breakthrough came through my ability to surrender and be vulnerable. Being strong doesn't mean that I'm immune to the trials and tribulations of life, but it gives me permission to laugh, cry, be angry, and love through it. My surrender depicted strength, not weakness. It was empowering and gave me such a sense of peace and serenity. What I realized is that fear is only what you make it. If you breathe life into fear, then you give fear power over you and your destiny. So face your fears and let fear know who has the power. As I mentioned earlier in this chapter, fear is a strategist. In order to beat a strategist at its own game, you must have a strategy of your own. Leaning on my faith provided me with a great strategy, which is to P.R.A.Y.

P – Be Present. Obstacles are placed in your life for a reason. These obstacles prepare you for what lies ahead. God makes sure that you receive the tools necessary to overcome your obstacles. This goes for your healing process as well. Once you have overcome your obstacles, you cannot continue to hold on to them. You cannot move forward while looking and focusing on the past. Let go of the past so that you can live for today.

R- Recognition. You must learn to recognize fear and its process in your life. There are some places and/or situations that are not conducive to your personal growth and development. Sometimes, we become complacent and will remain in places and/or situations for fear of the unknown. We also have to recognize when people in our lives are more of a hindrance than a help. There are people in your life that you may have to separate yourself from due to the fact that they are not meant to go with you to the next level.

A – Affirmation. Accept yourself for who you are. Each one of us was created to be unique. Remember, you are not born to just blend in, but to stand out. Your beauty is just that...your beauty. We tend to train our brains to focus on the negative versus the positive. Therefore, our perception of our self-image is tainted and our self-esteem is negatively affected. So today, choose to be more positive and enhance your self-esteem/self-image. Find 10 positive affirmations and repeat those affirmations to yourself on a daily basis. See if your outlook for the day improves as a result.

Y – Yes. What do you have to lose by following your hopes and dreams? The worst anyone can tell you is "no." Who are they to tell you, no? For if God is for you, who can be against you? What is for you, is for you. Your destiny is what you make it. You have a choice. You can sit back and wait for things to happen to you, or you can say yes, do the work, and claim what belongs to you. Bind your fears and walk BOLDLY into your full potential.

For all of the women/men reading this today, I pray that something was written or shared that helped you on this journey called life. I declare that chains will be broken. Whatever it is that is holding you back, I pray that you will be released from it. I declare that fear will no longer have any power or authority over your life. I pray that God will provide you with a clear vision and direction to walk into your full potential. Lord, I ask for a hedge of protection around your children as they move into their purpose. Touch their mind so that it may be open to new ideas, touch their ears so that they may hear your voice clearly, touch their mouths so that they may speak truth into the lives of others, and touch their hearts so that they may love themselves and each other freely. I pray for the healing of those who need to be healed. I pray for those who need comforting. I pray for those who may be lost, angry, or alone, that they may find their way back to you. Lord, I pray that your Spirit has its way within these stories so that these women/men may be touched, moved, and healed in Jesus' name. Amen.

1. How did fear challenge you in your life?

_____

_____

_____

_____

_____

2. How did fear hinder you from your breakthrough?

_____

_____

_____

_____

_____

ABUNDANCE
FOLLOWS YOU

WINNING IS IN
YOUR DNA

Bio

Pamela Knight is a psychotherapist and the founder of H.O.P.E Counseling and Consultation Services, LLC. She provides outpatient counseling for those struggling with various mental health issues (i.e. depression, anxiety, bipolar, etc.), behavioral problems, survivors of domestic violence/sexual abuse/rape, grief and loss, self-esteem, and marital/couples counseling. Pamela has a passion for helping others by instilling hope and promoting healing along this journey called life. She has made it her life's work to challenge others to get out of their own way so that they can develop and grow into the person that they are destined to be in this world. She believes that one should live their best life every day because tomorrow is not promised.

Pamela obtained her Bachelor of Arts degree in Psychology from Chowan College. She received her Master's degree in Counseling with an emphasis in Marriage and Family Therapy from East Tennessee State University. Pamela earned her doctorate degree in Counselor Education and Supervision from Regent University. She is dually licensed as a Licensed Professional Counselor and Licensed Marriage and Family Therapist in the state of Virginia.

LET THE
PROCESS
POSITION YOU

EXCUSES ARE PLANTED IN THE SOIL OF FEAR

Pearlean "Pe Flow" James

148

Dear Fear,

You did not take my joy. Despite the hurt that I experienced, I still look forward to living, laughing, and most of all, loving. Since I could remember, you have always told me to dim my light. Fear, you have made me feel awful for living in the joy that God has given me. You have encouraged me to hide the hurt that I have experienced by keeping secrets that should have been told. You told me to stay in situations even though I knew that I should have left a long time ago. Oh, but Fear...little did you know, no matter what I endured, the joy that I have could not be confined by something as deceitful as you. Fear, you did not win. This joy that I have will not be tampered with by you anymore.

Signed,

Joyful & Prosperous Pearlean Flowers James

Dear Fear,
You Can't Have My Joy

"Despite The Clouds, You Can Still Feel The Sun"

Fear: **F**inding **E**verything **A**larming and **R**isky

I used to think that the world around me was literally rainbows and glitter. I considered my mom to be superwoman because any time things got tough, I witnessed her get tougher. I considered my dad to be invincible because I'd seen him remain a respected and resourceful man in our community. My brothers were my protectors who made no mistakes in my eyes. At that time, I was the baby of the family and I felt like I had the best life a little girl in the hood could ask for. There were always family functions on Friday nights. Most of the family went to church together. The holidays were simply amazing, and I could not wait for them to come around. Although I had to study, school was easy and I had lots of friends. Every now and then, the family would have some tension or small situations would arise, but I would go right back to normal.

Despite the abnormalities in my upbringing, I chose to see the good in every situation since I accepted Christ at an early age. I thought anyone could make it out of any situation. I know one would think that this is a good thing; however, this frame of mind subjected me to some harsh realities. For example, I grew up in the hood and I planned to make it out because that's what my parents pushed me to do. However, I did not know that there were parents that did not want better for their children. In fact, I did not know that parents were allowed to have ill wishes toward their own flesh and blood.

By the time I hit high school, I started experiencing the different environments that I had been surrounded by all along. I started seeing the negative aspects of this world we live in. Although I was popular, I was still criticized for being myself. I was teased for following the rules my mother and father gave me. The rules were ordinary; however, I was amongst the few that actually followed them. I didn't drink, curse, sneak around with boys, etc. I was talked about for standing up for people who did not have the courage to stand up for themselves. I was judged because I did not wear the latest hairstyles or have on the most popular brands of clothes. Heck, at one point, I was picked on for being a positive, happy teenager. After a while, I began to put my guard up, and for a good while, my heart hardened. I was tired of being the underdog. I was tired of being the target of someone else's frustration. I was afraid that I was going to lose my happiness… my joy. I had to protect myself, and the only way I knew was to become guarded.

As a result, I became a version of myself that I did not know existed. I started to be a mean girl. Now if you know me, you would have been like there is not a mean bone in your body. Oh, but there were plenty. At that time, I let the fear of being hurt allow me to hurt others. I was going to hurt you before you hurt me. I was the person that says, "I'm going to be brutally honest." That was the furthest statement from the truth. What I meant was, I was going to use your vulnerability to hurt you with the attempt of making me feel better about myself. For so long, this was my normal. Honestly, this version of me developed because of the many times others made me feel awful for being happy. I internalized that and said, "Well, maybe they will be happy with me being mean." At that time, I was tired of being hurt, wanted to belong somewhere, and cared entirely too much about what others thought of me.

My true intentions were well hidden. Each day, I struggled with who I was as a person. I knew that on the inside, I was this sweet, carefree, and loving person. But, how do you show that when you are afraid of being hurt continuously by everyone? Over time, God began to nudge me. I became tired of being in such a negative space. I felt miserable! Every day that I woke up, I wanted to hide from the world. I lost myself. I lost Pearl. My personal demise showed in how I dressed, who I talked to, and in the activities that I participated in. I had fully engaged in "operation hide from the world." I dressed to fade into the background. I began to isolate myself from all family, friends, and loved ones. All I did was go to work, school, and church. With this routine, I denied fear the chance of hurting me. Hey, if I don't talk to anyone, then no one can hurt me. I mean, I loved myself; therefore, I wouldn't hurt myself, right?

In this season of personal isolation, I found "love" and I thought that I would finally be rescued from the negative space that I had been in. However, that was not the case. In what I believed to be my healing grace, I became more broken. As I think about it, that is when I became the most lost. I had graduated from high school, fell in love with the "perfect guy" and was on my way to college. College was amazing; however, the "perfect guy" became not so perfect after about 7 months. During this time, I started losing myself even more because I was trying to be what he said he wanted me to be. "Dress this way, speak this way, eat this, don't talk to them," he said. Despite the warning signs, I still married him. Yes, you read that right. I married him. Why? I was afraid of going to hell! Who wants to burn in the lake of fire for all eternity? As Christians, we are taught "no sex before marriage." So, in my mind, this one act of "sin" weighed more than the other acts of sin. In actuality, it does not; however, I did not learn this until I started studying the Bible on my own.

I actually thought that marrying him would make my life better. It did, but only for about three months. The rest of that year, I cried. I mean ugly cried, every day. However, the fear of failure made me stay. I thought to myself, *no way I would let my marriage fail.* You see, so many people told me that my marriage would not work because was too young to get married (I was 19). While I still do not believe that statement, they were right. My fear came true. My marriage failed before it started. Unfortunately, I stayed in the marriage because I was afraid of the "I told you so!"

Even though I stayed, I started asking God for a way out. I did not want any regrets. I loved him so much that I would rather him be happy, and I just be content. Unbeknownst to me, I continued to put the need to please others at the forefront. Once again, I was afraid that I would hurt him; therefore, I was willing to allow him to keep hurting me. Thus, I stayed. I stayed. Each day was extreme turmoil. As a result, I began to resent the One who had been carrying me through this entire experience. I started questioning God. *Why me?* I truly believed that I had done everything the way my parents had taught me. Yet, I still ended up here; broken, busted, humiliated, ashamed and beaten down. At that moment, I decided that going forward, I was going to live life differently. Forget the morals and values that I had been taught and grown to care so much about. Life was going to be different. I was angry! I was determined not to get hurt anymore.

I walked away with nothing. I left everything. I didn't even want the expensive china that was gifted to us as a wedding gift. I left with only some of my clothes. Eventually, I didn't need them. Heck, I was dressing like an old maid at that point anyway. Disconnecting from such a toxic situation encouraged me to leave everything behind. I felt an immediate release after that physical disconnect; however, it wouldn't be for several more months that a divorce would officially happen.

Around this time, I began to become reacquainted with my, now husband. He knew the version of me that did not take risks and did everything that was "morally right." However, he was in for a treat. Upon getting reacquainted, I boldly told him, "That's the old me. There's a new Pearl in town." Everything was up for grabs. So, we hit the ground running. We did everything society tells you not to do in a new relationship. The biggest of those things was sex before marriage. I would be lying if I told you that it did not feel good. Heck! This new way of doing things felt amazing. I was angry with God, so I had to prove to Him that I could do this without him.

Even throughout my rebellion, God still had his hands on me. He had sent me my forever. It was at that moment of realization that I became most convicted of how angry I was with God. He knew my heart and yet He still decided to bless me abundantly. He knew that the root of my anger was fear. Even through all those trials, God had never left nor forsaken me. No matter how hurt and broken I became when I could no longer go through life on my own, God accepted me back with open arms. I had to be redesigned and recharged. Thus, finally, I began to listen to God. At this point, I was so tired. He showed me that I was being ungrateful for taking the gift of joy, that He gave me, and burying it so that no one could use it against me. As I started to feel completely convicted, God started to heal my heart. It wasn't easy. You know, healing hurts sometimes. It hurts because you have to let go of the negative ties that you have developed with people and/or situations. That can be difficult because it's much easier to hold on to hurt than it is to forgive, accept your participation in the ordeal and move on. Despite the uneasy transition, I noticed that I yearned to be happy like I use to be. I noticed that I took pride in helping others find their joy despite their situations.

Believe me, you can have joy in all situations. I was going through a divorce and people around me could not understand why I was so gleeful. It was nothing but God. Now, when I got married, I did not think it would end up being dissolved; however, I realized that I did not allow God to lead me when I made the decision to get married. I later learned that marriage needed to happen. I needed to go through the fire. I needed the fire so that I could be molded into what God wanted me to be. As you can tell, I do not regret the decision to get married. I mean, think about it. Any time you fail, you usually remember what to do to get it right the next time. That failed marriage helped me become the woman and wife that I am today. Thus, failure did not win; neither did fear. I knew that I was created to love and that God was preparing me for greater.

Despite all that I had going on, I learned that I could live in this world but not be of this world. There is so much going on; but, I can still bask in the gift of joy that God blessed me with. That does not mean that I am not sympathetic to others, it just means that I am walking in my truth. I learned that you do not have to be around people that are in the same situation that you are in. I want you to know that by nature, we tend to place ourselves with people that have similarities; however, I learned that it is beneficial to surround yourself with individuals that challenge you and you challenge them. Growth happens in the challenge! Do not let fear get the satisfaction of telling you that challenge isn't necessary. It is very necessary. It's necessary because that is where your growth will become activated. I learned to appreciate joy! Happiness is a conditional emotion that changes depending upon your situation. However, joy is a divine gift from God. Despite the situation, the joy of the Lord is present in your spirit.

Anytime you are going through a rough situation and you are still able to genuinely smile through it, just know that is the joy of the Lord. Through all the heartache and pain, the gift of joy is what kept me going. I am forever grateful that God blessed me with such a gift. I may have fumbled joy, locked joy up, and even tried to bury joy, but God's grace allowed my heart to maintain such a beautiful gift. Now, my joy remains activated despite what is going on in the world around me.

When I decided to be an author in Dear Fear, fear tried to come back for me. I had to plow my way through a very dark place because fear almost took my joy. I was devastated. How dare fear to have the audacity to still try to remain relevant in my life. This must be a joke. But, it wasn't. However, as I found my way out, my appreciation of joy became more evident.

No matter what you are going through, the key word is *through* (because you will make it out), let the fact that you will make it out enable your state of joy! Trouble does not last always. I mean, think about it. Even when you don't see the sun through the clouds, it's still giving off heat. This means that life is still being manifested!

1. **What does joy mean to you and when was a time fear deprived you of joy?**

_____

_____

_____

_____

_____

2. **Now, what are you going to do to make sure you don't lose your joy?**

_____

_____

_____

_____

_____

BIGGER AND BETTER IS HERE

Bio

Pearlean Flowers James is a wife, mother, daughter, sister, best friend, educator, basketball coach, and just an all around beautiful soul. She is happy 99.9% of the time and she loves love. She enjoys singing, dancing, serving, and giving love. Relationship discussions are her guilty pleasures. Pearlean was once told that she could get more information from people than the FBI. Food for the spirit and body are always a brightener on a gloomy day. She enjoys seeing others experiencing the joy that she was blessed with.

YOUR NEW THING
GOD HAS FOR YOU IS
ON THE OTHER SIDE
OF FEAR

YOUR BEST LIFE IS ON THE OTHER SIDE OF FEAR

Tamika TJ Woodard

Dear Fear,

I remember when I was 10 years old and you set in for the first time. I remember the tears, the shame, and the silence. I remember asking myself why I didn't speak up. Why didn't I make it stop? This is when I remember severing ties with my voice. She went her way, and I went mine. I was left feeling betrayed, feeling that she had let me down. She did. She tried to come back many times after. I didn't understand why, because all she would do is abandon me the first chance she got, over and over again, just like the others. She would be no different from the men and the relationships I've had. No different from the friends (and sometimes even my family), along with my courage, my confidence, and my power that would all abandon me as well. You became my new best friend. Who needed a voice with a friend like you, Fear? You made me see how useless my voice was. You were good at your job. You deceived me.

I don't know if you have a friend like this in your life but if you do, be sure to check her immediately because she's like a bad virus. She will destroy everything good like you tried to do to me. You destroyed my relationships and attempted to destroy my family, my jobs and my sanity. You also tried to steal my joy, my dreams, and my life. It was 3 years ago when I decided enough was enough. I was tired of losing. I was tired of hurting. I was tired of hiding. So, I decided to take a stand by speaking out and using my voice to expose you for exactly what you are. You have gotten away for far too long, and now I'm coming back for everything you stole from me.

I know that when you leave one place you always look for another space to occupy. You are slick and will infiltrate minds without anyone even realizing it. So I'm warning each reader to take this letter as notice to stand their ground; guard their mind, their heart, and most importantly use their voice. Speak out. Affirm those things you know to be true and good. Call out those things that are not. Be bold and confident. Be your true authentic self. Be the Queen God created you to be. I know I am and you can too!

Signed,

TJ Woodard

YOUR WINNING SEASON IS ON THE OTHER SIDE OF FEAR

YOUR NEXT LEVEL
HAS SO MUCH
POWER ATTACHED
TO IT

Dear Fear,
You Can't Have My Voice

I am Tamika, but you can call me TJ. Many know me as a mother, daughter, friend, entrepreneur, mentor, and author. What they don't know, is that I am a little girl hiding behind a woman who lost her voice somewhere around the age of 10 due to molestation.

I was born in North Carolina but raised in Southeast DC. When I tell people that, they find it hard to believe because they say I don't look or sound like a girl from the "ghetto." They say I don't roll my neck, or have that "angry black woman" attitude. They say I actually enunciate my words, or in other words, I talk proper. Well let me tell you this, I don't look or sound like a lot of things, which is why I am sharing my story today. I have perfected deceiving people by only showing them what I wanted them to see, when deep down inside I have spent the last 30 years hiding secrets from my past that I have so conveniently tried to forget and subconsciously locked away, vowing to never, ever discuss. I call myself an introvert, but honestly, it is an excuse I used to justify why I have been unable to use my voice. It has allowed me to retreat, hiding behind the confident person that others see and the broken little girl that has yet to heal from her past. Past, meaning things that were done by others and things I have allowed others to get away with for fear of what would happen if I finally used my voice. *Who would listen? Who would be hurt or angry? Who would sympathize? Who would understand? Who would protect her? Who would blame her? Who would believe her?* These were questions that would arise bringing me back to that place of silence.

Being mishandled, in any way, tends to shape the way you view life and relationships. It causes you to question who you are and your self-worth. I took responsibility for something that was done to me that wasn't mine to take on. This is one way fear can creep into your life like it did mine. What fear did was step in at that moment of weakness and led me to believe that, at the time, I should have spoken up for myself; my voice let me down. I blamed myself and felt that I did something that left me in silence, without a voice. So here's my journey to finding my voice.

It was around 10 years old that I first remember my voice leaving me and fear moving in. It was right after the molestation that set the precedence of fear silencing me, in a way that my life would forever be changed. It was living with the knowledge that when my boyfriend thought it was my "first time" it really wasn't. Someone had taken that from me. From that time on, I was made to believe that people could take whatever they wanted from me and there was nothing I could say or do about it. Fear took over. Fear took residence, and where my voice once lived, fear now took occupancy. But no, fear did not come alone; along with it came guilt, shame, embarrassment, anger, disappointment, rejection, and abandonment, which would change the way I viewed relationships and the way I viewed myself. On the day my voice left, it didn't leave alone. My voice was the scapegoat for fear, taking everything of value because she knew that if I truly understood what I had in me, that even the hurtful things I would experience would later be used to propel me into my purpose. She knew that even if she didn't know how much these things were worth, eventually those who truly got to know me would know. So, fear silenced my voice and proceeded to take away my self-esteem, self-love, self-worth, and self-confidence. The way I see it, she was quite "self"ish only taking the things she thought she could barter later. Things she felt were powerful, and if used properly, could one day be the thing that would change lives.

Fear stealing my voice came with a price. It was as if my voice left, but would show up whenever she

wanted. She taunted me as she stood in the wings, only stepping up for small things or when I would need her to protect or help others, even those who didn't deserve it. She was good at giving advice, as long as it wasn't anything pertaining to her situation. She would master disappearing whenever I needed her to step in on my behalf, primarily during times when I was being used or abused and taken advantage of. Oh, how convenient! I only wish I had the same luxury. Maybe I did. I don't know. It was as if I was living with dissociative disorder, which is why I refer to my voice as "she" or "her." My voice would act as if it had a mind of its own. Whenever I didn't want to face something, fear would step in and my voice would leave. Fear would rescue me from having to face difficult situations, causing me to ignore them as if the problem would go away. Sometimes it did, but sometimes it would come back with a vengeance or even escalate into a bigger problem. Whenever it was something that I was comfortable with, my voice would *conveniently* come back loud and strong. There was no schedule or routine, but more like a pop-up shop, whenever the timing was good for her.

This became "our thing." Our little song and dance. After the first time, it was almost automatic. I would lose my voice and fear would step in. It became a vicious cycle, creating a life of mental, emotional and even sexual abuse all self-inflicted as a result of the abandonment left behind when my voice would sit quietly as disappointment settled in. I remember times when I was so angry at my voice because I knew I needed to say something, but it was as if fear was in the driver's seat. *Stop. No. I don't want to. I don't like it,* would all be thoughts, but rarely could I formulate the words when it came to me speaking up. I would find myself doing things I didn't want to do, and not doing things I wanted to do, all because I didn't know how to effectively and confidently use the voice that God had given me.

It's amazing how it doesn't even seem like my voice has aged. It's as if she is stuck at the tender age of

10. Although I'm in my forties and quite mature for my age, sometimes I still feel like I'm that same

10-year-old little girl. I'm often told that I seem younger than I am, mainly because of the low, bashful tone of my voice. Yes, a voice that can be strong and powerful when she wants to be, but more frequently fearful, nervous and shy. My voice, I guess we can give her a name. Let's call her Miss T. Yes, I like that. In Miss T's defense, she has witnessed a lot. I'm a little concerned about my voice, to be honest, because of the things she's seen and the secrets that she has held on to for so long. I don't know how anyone could survive after that. But I did. She has witnessed and experienced so much abuse; mental, physical and emotional. Maybe even spiritual.

My voice was there even during my periods of sexual promiscuity, two failed marriages, single parenting, job loss, being used and abused, bouts with anxiety and even during my times of thoughts of suicide and depression. She remembered all too well, often reflecting back to its origin and sitting silently in the background.

Miss T (my voice) represents so many things. In this story, she represents my inability to protect myself from abuse. It has caused me to doubt myself even in the times when I was confident enough to speak up but instead remained quiet. It's about how I have allowed fear to take control of my voice preventing me from being the person I was created by God to be. A Queen. It is how my voice would always show up to protect others but would abandon me when I needed to protect myself. It represents watching my mother be physically abused without being able to help her. It is about constantly subjecting myself to being used and abused because I didn't use my voice to speak up and speak out. It represents the guilt and shame that I have carried for far too long.

As I take this journey to self-discovery, I am finding that voice. I am becoming more vocal. I have not

shared everything, but I am getting there. Fear did not just take over my voice, it took over my life. It didn't just cripple me at 10, but for many years to follow. I missed out on my entire high school experience and many pivotal moments in my life because I was ashamed people would see me and know those things I said I would never share. I did not succeed in certain jobs and passed up opportunities because of my fear of speaking up; fear of feeling unworthy, not good enough, not smart enough and not pretty enough.

Today, I am continuing to speak out for all the little girls like myself who have lost their voice due to abuse, divorce, abandonment, rejection, teenage pregnancy, sexual assault and other things that make us believe that we should sit silently while fear becomes the front runner. Now in my forties, 3 children and 2 divorces later, I am finding my voice again. I started a mentorship program called Queen Series because I spent 30 years too long hiding behind my fears. Silenced. My voice was masked by a façade of who I portrayed myself to be. The smile, makeup, and the clothes did not reveal the little girl without the voice. I lost so much time in my life that I could have truly been happy and I did not want this to be the fate of another young girl, or anyone for that matter. No longer will fear hold me back. So as I speak out and continue to share my story, I say FEAR, YOU CAN'T HAVE MY VOICE!

1. **Is there a time where you should have used your voice and you chose not to? How did that make you feel?**

_____

_____

_____

_____

_____

2. **We all have a story. Which part of your story has fear kept you from sharing?**

_____

_____

_____

_____

_____

3. There is power in your words. What affirmations will you use to speak positivity in your life and allow you to help others?

_____

_____

_____

_____

_____

RESTORATION
IS HERE

Bio

Tamika Woodard is the oldest of four siblings and is a mother and grandmother. She comes with many gifts and talents, but most importantly a heart to serve and help others achieve their goals. She is also a newly published author and motivational speaker. She recently published her first book titled *A Queen's Guide to Dating the Christian Way*, a book that provides godly principles for dating God's way but also stresses the importance of having a relationship with him allowing God to truly bless us with the great things he has for us. She has survived a life of hardships and struggle and knows first-hand how to rise above obstacles that come before her.

God has had his hand on her life carrying her through each and every situation she has had to endure. Tamika is the founder of Queens Series, a program in which she mentors young women between the ages of 15 - 25, offering advice and education on self-love, self-respect, self-esteem, love, and relationships. She motivates, inspires and encourages all those who come into her path to keep God first and to walk in their true and divine purpose.

Tamika understands how her personal experiences have taught her so many things, but most importantly how she is an overcomer and that she is the daughter of a King. She hopes that her desire to mentor women and men of all ages will show that no matter the struggle, no matter the circumstances, no matter what they have been through, they too can overcome. For their future, the possibilities are endless if they don't quit and keep God first!

GOD IS ACTIVATING PLACES IN YOU THAT THE ENEMY TRIED TO LAY DORMANT

YOUR PURPOSE IS POWERFUL

Priscilla McNealy

Dear Fear,

I used to allow you to hold me captive. I allowed you to convince me that I was not worthy or good enough. You comforted me by telling me that staying stagnant was the best thing that I could do; not only for myself, but for my children as well. You told me that it was okay to allow another person to abuse me mentally, physically, and emotionally. You told me that it was okay to hide and avoid confrontation instead of standing up for what I believe in. Fear, you sold me many a dream. As long as I continued to buy those dreams, you held me captive.

I'm writing you right now to tell you that I see through your lies, attempts to comfort me, and those dreams you've been selling me. I do deserve more. My children deserve even more. We deserve for me to put my best foot forward, give it all I've got and maximize myself in every single area of my life.

I know you won't leave me alone, which is why I'm ready for this fight. I know you won't give up on me too easily, but I am ready. Greatness is on the inside of me, and I refuse to allow you to keep me captive any longer!

Bring it on,
Priscilla McNealy

DON'T ALLOW
FEAR TO HINDER
YOUR FREEDOM

STOP HAVING SIDE CONVERSATIONS WITH FEAR

Dear Fear,
You Can't Have My Will to Live

Have you ever heard of a person who seemed to have split personalities? Well, I was that type of woman. At one point and time in my life, I possessed many different versions of myself. I felt as if I was putting on an act as a result of the different hats that I wear in my life. One moment I am a national guardswoman, then a sign language instructor, and then a mom who attends every event that her children have at their schools. The next thing you know, I am this woman who cannot stop crying or get out of bed. I was taught very early in life to hide behind my smile. When others find out about bits and pieces of my testimony, they are always shocked and say, "You don't look like what you've been through!" Hiding behind my smile is all I knew how to do.

When you're a child who is constantly being abused mentally, emotionally, and physically by someone who brought you into this world, sometimes hiding behind your smile is all you know how to do. I had this fear of being judged and viewed as weak, so I suppressed the elements of my situation. At the time, I felt I was doing myself and the world a favor by not sharing my troubles.

In addition to those experiences, I was torn between two identities: The Hearing world, and the Deaf world. You see, both of my parents are Deaf and sign language is my first language. The Deaf world call their hearing children CODAs (Child of a Deaf Adult). This silent world is all I knew until I started kindergarten and had to endure speech therapy because I was almost labeled as having a speech impairment. I had to learn English (correct English, that is) at the age of five when everyone else in my class already knew the language. Imagine what a little black girl in an elementary school in the small city of Dothan, Alabama, would experience at this delicate time in her life. I was lost. I was bullied. I didn't know who I was. So, I did what I knew best; smile and keep it moving. Afraid of the consequences of confronting the kids who bullied me, I held my head down and pretended that I did not hear them. I was not just afraid of the consequences that I would receive from the school, but from my mother as well.

I put my smiley-face on for most of my life, up until a few years ago. While doing so, I also had to carry the pain and burdens of the oppression and discrimination I saw my Deaf parents experience. It angered me that such injustice could be done to someone just because they could not hear. Now, imagine adding the fact that we are people of color as well; my parents had two strikes against them. Not just my parents, but just about every Black Deaf person in Dothan, AL. Being the oldest of my siblings, my mom took me everywhere with her. You could say that naturally, I was her "little interpreter." I remember buying houses and cars (interpreting for my parents) all before the age of 10. As a young teenager, I recall being in courtrooms interpreting cases for my parents. Today, I know that all of this is totally unethical, but back then, I am pretty sure the laws that mandated sign language interpreting were not being enforced. All of these experiences played a major role that shaped me into being the woman that I am today. The pain that I saw my parents go through resulted in the birth of my business, which is a nationwide company that provides the very services that my parents needed back then.

Who would have known or even thought of such a thing? Not I! But God did. I had fears of moving forward with my business. Insecurity and the need for approval from others will do that to you. Feeling inferior to white interpreters who appeared to be more successful and talented than me rocked me to my core. Most of these interpreters became interpreters simply because they thought that sign language was "cool." For me, sign language is my life. It is hard to explain the concept of my fear, but I can tell you that these interpreters intimidated me. I felt like an imposter.

Let's backtrack to the abuse. When I tell you that abuse can cause you to feel so low, so unloved, and so worthless, I mean it. The abuse I endured caused me to date men that didn't mean me no good (incorrect grammar intended), and the sad part is, I knew it! But it was as if I was stuck in this fog of self-loathing and refusing to honor, love, and respect myself. I found myself married to a man that loved marijuana, created songs that degraded women and loved his boys more than he loved me. Have you ever heard of a woman that thought they could change a man? Yep, I was one of them. I married a man that I thought *if I loved him hard enough, he would love me back and switch up his priorities.* Boy, was I wrong. I was suicidal and miserable, and because of my immature relationship with God, I was afraid that he'd strike me down with lightning if left my then husband without proof of his infidelity.

Eventually, I caught him cheating via the infamous Facebook Messenger. I got my .45, called my girl, walked into our bedroom where he was sleeping, and told her that I was going to kill my husband tonight. At that moment, I'd had enough. I was tired of not feeling accepted, tired of the pain I harbored from the abuse I endured as a child, and especially tired of him taking me for granted. My friend tried to talk me out of it, and while she was trying to calm me down, I charged my .45 and aimed it at his head. When I got ready to pull the trigger, I saw that my then 1 ½-year-old son was asleep with him. Had my son not moved his tiny little arms, I would have shot and killed his father. I realized then that I allowed rage and anger to control me. I almost committed murder and could have brought harm to my baby. I went back into the living room where the evidence was displayed, and oddly enough, I felt as if a gigantic burden had been released from my shoulders. I felt as if I could breathe, and most importantly, I felt at peace. The next day he moved out, and I felt so free.

For those of you who know me personally, you know that this is when I developed the "royal mentality." I vowed that I would never again be so dependent on the love and approval of a man. From that moment forward, I knew whose I was and that I didn't have to beg for someone's love, let alone try to change them. I deserved better, and my children deserved better. I learned to love and value myself. I realized that I am God's royalty regardless of how my abuser viewed me, how the world saw me with my "weird Deaf parents that flop their hands around to communicate," and how my ex-husband saw me.

I am God's beloved, and when I learned to embrace His love, I learned to cherish my own life. I also learned to become a better mother and give my children the relationship that I never had. I'm going to be straight forward with you. It took a while for this newfound love to settle in. Even after my divorce, I still slipped up and attracted men that meant me no good. However, this time around, I knew when to cut them off. I saw the red flags and knew to get ghost really quick. It took time and me learning to truly love myself to learn how to move forward and not be held captive by fear. For a while though, I was a woman who smiled to the public but was an angry black woman fussing about everything wrong behind closed doors. I was a mess; an ugly mess.

After realizing that I was an ugly mess, I got even more depressed and texted those who were close to me and told them that I had enough of life and that I could not take it anymore. I turned my phone off and planned to get the .45 my husband had and end my life. The next thing I know, two officers from the Pelham Police Department (we now reside in Pelham, AL) were at my door and told me that two friends from Dothan were concerned about my text and called the police. I was so depressed that I wasn't even moved by that notion. I still wanted to end my life. As a result, I was admitted to the hospital. I had 7 whole days to realize that my life was worth living.

I'm here to tell you that grace, love, and mercy go a long way. When I saw that I was allowing the past to repeat itself, I cried out to God and asked him to please help me. I did not want to be a bitter woman or mother to my precious children. God answered my cries immediately. All he said was one word: "Forgive." That one word almost knocked the life out of me. It was as if I was wrestling with the devil himself. My flesh did not want to let go of all of the burdens and pain of the past. It was all I knew. I was afraid of what it would feel like to let go of the pain. *What would I feel after I let go?* My spirit thought otherwise. I had to dig deep and write a letter to every person that I needed to forgive. It felt good. It was as if all of the layers of pain were being peeled off of me. Doing so was a form of physical, mental, and emotional therapy. In addition, I sought out a therapist to help me sort out the pieces I had suppressed deep down in my memory and behind my infamous front of a smile. To this day, I am continuously purging the memories that come forth and boy does it feel good to have more layers peeled off!

I never thought that I would be able to forgive and literally forget so that I could move on. The love that now flows out of me to my children feels so good and I know that they are happy to have their mama being free of pain and hurt. Regardless of the hurt you are holding on to, you need to know that it is possible to let go and give it all to God. He wants to take it from you so you can be who He has called you to be. Your life is a testimony, imagine the power of your story. Imagine the lives you can and will change and save! Imagine the effects of working in your calling. The best part of letting go is that you'll find yourself being used by God and encouraging others, all while finding yourself being encouraged too.

Have you ever heard of a person who brushes compliments off because they do not believe them or they think they are being made fun of in an indirect way? Well, I used to be that woman, too. Low confidence and self-esteem will do that to you. I never used to believe people when they told me that I was such a strong person or that I was beautiful. When I hear those words now, I embrace them; especially when they tell me their perspective of my being strong. I realized that I really am strong because I was strong enough to accept my past and be healed of it. I was strong enough to self-admit myself to a hospital and get the help that I needed. Most importantly, I was strong enough to stay alive and be here with my family.

Reader, your life is precious. Never allow situations and

circumstances to make you think otherwise. You are here for a reason. God put you here on this earth for a very special reason. We are not worthy of His love, but we sure are worth it to Him! If you're reading this book right now, you are proof. Proof that you are immersed in love, grace, and mercy. Every breath that you take and every step that you take matters. I cannot stress enough that you matter. For so many years, I felt more worthless than a piece of gum stuck on the bottom of a shoe! I didn't think I mattered! Being beaten until your skin tears and bleeds and having things thrown at you by someone who is supposed to love and nurture you can do some serious damage. I am proof that the damage can be undone. Sometimes we go through things that will help us become a better version of us. The love that I have for my children brings me so much joy, knowing that I am bringing them up in the complete opposite way than I was brought up.

Are you holding a grudge? Is there a relationship that you need to end? Who or what is stopping you from being all that God has called you to be? We all come from different walks of life, but one thing is for absolute sure: You cannot move forward if you do not forgive. Imagine yourself voluntarily agreeing to be enslaved. This is what holding on to pain and refusing to forgive feels like. You are God's beloved! You have a choice to be bound in the captivity of unforgiveness. You decide whether or not it gives you power. As my coach always tells me, "You have to give God your unconditional yes!" What will it be for you? To be free or held in bondage? It's your decision!

1. Do you love yourself to the point that you will not allow anyone or anything to take away your peace of mind and sanity?

_____

_____

_____

_____

_____

2. Do you love yourself enough to the point that you can look fear in the face and tell it to go back to the pits of hell?

_____

_____

_____

_____

_____

PIVOT INTO PURPOSE

FEAR IS A LIAR

Bio

Priscilla McNealy is a mother of four, a member of the Army National Guard, and she is the CEO and founder of Royal Signs Interpreting Agency. She is also a CODA (Child of a Deaf Adult). Because she was born into the Deaf world, sign language was her first language. As a CODA, she saw her Deaf parents experience both discrimination and oppression. Priscilla realized that the primary reason her parents were experiencing this was that there was a lack of knowledge about Deaf culture. Her mission is to educate people and entities that being Deaf is not a disability, it is a lifestyle. As a result, she founded Royal Signs Interpreting Agency and is on a mission to bridge the communication gap between the Deaf and Hearing communities. There are over 70 million Deaf people in the world who are more than worth connecting to. Not only does Royal Signs provide interpreting services and teach American Sign Language, but RSI also helps corporate brands increase their loyal customer base and their revenue by tapping into an untouched market and provide training, captioning and transcription services as well as keynote messages at events. Royal Signs has worked with brands such as The Clinton Foundation, U.S. Department of Homeland Security, The United States Postal Service, and National American Miss. When Priscilla is not busy running Royal Signs Interpreting and serving her country, she enjoys traveling with her family.

STOP ALLOWING
FEAR TO ABUSE
YOU

MAKE THE BOLD,
COURAGEOUS &
CONSCIOUS DECISION
TO FEAR. LESS.
EVERYDAY

DearFearBook.Com

Made in the USA
Columbia, SC
18 April 2019